CLASSIC PHILOS~~OPHY FOR THE~~
MODERN ~~MAN~~

Andrew Lynn has a Ph.D. in Renaissance literature from Cambridge University. He has lectured in Western civilization in Beijing and now practises law with a particular interest in the field of international dispute resolution.

www.andrewlynn.com

Classic Philosophy for the Modern Man

Andrew Lynn

HOWGILL
HOUSE

Howgill House Books

www.howgillhousebooks.com

Copyright © Andrew Lynn 2017

ISBN 978-1-912360-03-1

CONTENTS

INTRODUCTION

How to live well?

There is no more important question than this.

The difficulty is not in finding an answer. Everybody (and their dog) is willing to give you an answer. But the answer they give is invariably *their* answer. It may be the answer reflecting their particular prejudices and preoccupations at this particular time. It may be the answer pointing in the direction of their particular commercial or political objectives. Or it may simply be the answer most widely circulated and – seemingly at least – widely accepted by the public at large.

This is where philosophy steps in as the boldest attempt to establish generally applicable principles for living well. Confident that philosophy at its best reaches further and probes deeper than other approaches to the great questions of life, we give you here a readable and thought-provoking selection from classic works of the very best thinkers from European, Asian, and American history. We start in the West with Plato, Aristotle, and Marcus Aurelius and in the East with Chuang-tzu – each of whom provides fundamental rules for living and acting. From there we journey to Italy and Spain of the Renaissance where Machiavelli, Castiglione, and Gracián teach us how to obtain and exercise power, how to live gracefully, and how to advance in the world. Northern Europe is the next destination: from Germany, Nietzsche teaches nobility of soul, and from England William Hazlitt anatomizes success. Our final destination, fittingly, is the New World, from where Ralph Waldo Emerson speaks to us of the importance of being one's own man. Between them, these profound and inspirational thinkers tell a story of mankind's tussles with his predicament and provide solutions to a wide variety of his problems.

'The unexamined life is not worth living,' said Socrates famously, in a saying that has constituted the fundamental self-justification of many a professional and armchair philosopher. There is much to be said for a life lived in the unremitting pursuit of truth. These words are not, however, an unambiguous confirmation of the life of the mind. Socrates uttered them not in a moment of calm reflection but at his trial for corruption of Athenian youth and for impiety, having been found guilty and condemned to death by drinking hemlock. While the unexamined life is not worth living, then, might not the *over*-examined life be unliveable too?

This book, accordingly, charts a middle path between the life of the mind and life in this world.

We are at all times interested in *practical* wisdom. Academic philosophy as taught in universities is remote from our concerns – too much of it is pedantic, dry, and sterile. What you hold in your hands is a handbook for living: it is an account of how the greatest minds have spoken to us on how to grow and prosper as flesh-and-blood human beings. This they do, and they do with originality and panache. There will be no need for drinking of hemlock here.

Underlying and reconciling the many diverse approaches contained in this book is a single guiding principle that is best summed up in the phrase 'self-possession'. Self-possession is what is needed to escape the unrealities of Plato's cave and it is what is needed to achieve Aristotle's golden mean. Self-possession in its various forms is what is needed to be an effective emperor (Marcus Aurelius), prince (Machiavelli), courtier (Castiglione), and man of the world (Gracián). The noble soul of Nietzsche and Emerson's self-trusting man are marked by precisely the same quality.

You will be inspired and changed by these texts. They bear within them the possibility of new ways of thinking and living. They are the works of great beings speaking to us across the centuries.

Hear them. Listen to them. Let them in.

PLATO, THE REPUBLIC

INTRODUCTION

It has been said that the history of Western philosophy is but a footnote to Plato. It could equally well be said that all of Plato is but an elaboration of his 'allegory of the cave'. The allegory of the cave – from Book VII of his *Republic* – is a dialogue between Socrates, Plato's teacher, and Plato's brother Glaucon. It is a profound reflection on the world of unreality – what the Eastern religions call 'maya' – in which we live.

We are first to imagine human beings living in an underground den. Their legs and necks have been chained so that they cannot move and can only see what is in front of them. Behind these prisoners – at a distance – a fire is blazing. Between the fire and the prisoners is a low wall. Across the top of the wall, men carry vessels, statues, and figures of animals. Some of these men are talking and their voices echo off the cave walls.

What, then, would be the experience of these prisoners and how would they understand their own world? Of themselves, they would see nothing but their own shadows cast against the cave wall. Of the objects carried along the wall, they would likewise see merely shadowed forms. And of the talk of the men in the cave, they would hear only the echo, which to them would seem to emanate from the shadows on the wall. Their whole truth and reality would be nothing but this shadowy puppet-show.

Now imagine one of the prisoners is released and is able to make an escape. He will be pained and distressed by the brightness of the natural light flowing in from the mouth of the cave. He will still believe that the shadows that he formerly saw are truer than the objects he is being shown now. At first, he will stay with the shadows and reflections. Then he will venture out at night-time. Only at the end will he be able to behold the sun as the source of all that is.

Finally, imagine what would happen if the released man decided to liberate his fellow prisoners. He would have to return to the cave below to do that. Now, though, his sight would be unaccustomed to the darkness. To the prisoners below – who have been busy conferring honours upon those who were 'quickest to observe the passing shadows and to remark which of them went before, and which followed after' – the returned man with his ineffective vision would seem ridiculous. Better not to even think of ascending, they would conclude. And, should anyone think of releasing another – well, let him be killed.

Plato gives his own interpretation of the allegory: the prison-house, he says, is 'the world of sight'. We are trapped, then, in an illusory world created by the senses and condemned to see only the shadows of true reality. Academic philosophers at this juncture invariably refer to Plato's theory of Forms. The Forms are the unchanging essences – such as beauty, truth, courage, and goodness – that support the ever-varying particular manifestations of themselves. It is these and these alone that have true substantial reality.

There's nothing wrong with that explanation. But Plato's allegory is just as much concerned with what can be called 'the experience of awakening'. It tells of how easy it is to become trapped in a false world without knowing it: all that is required for us to go along with the fiction is for the components of the false world to appear consistent with each other. It tells of the process of awakening, which is impeded and interrupted by bouts of pain and denial. And it tells of the alienation and isolation of the awakened one from his fellow men. Far from conferring glory or honour, the returning truth-bearer is perceived as defective and inadequate. The rewards of awakening are not easily shared. And yet those rewards are real – the power to act rationally both in public and in private life.

BOOK VII

And now, I said, let me show in a figure how far our nature is enlightened or unenlightened:—Behold! human beings living in a underground den, which has a mouth open towards the light and reaching all along the den; here they have been from their childhood, and have their legs and necks chained so that they cannot move, and can only see before them, being prevented by the chains from turning round their heads. Above and behind them a fire is blazing at a distance, and between the fire and the prisoners there is a raised way; and you will see, if you look, a low wall built along the way, like the screen which marionette players have in front of them, over which they show the puppets.

I see.

And do you see, I said, men passing along the wall carrying all sorts of vessels, and statues and figures of animals made of wood and stone and various materials, which appear over the wall? Some of them are talking, others silent.

You have shown me a strange image, and they are strange prisoners.

Like ourselves, I replied; and they see only their own shadows, or the shadows of one another, which the fire throws on the opposite wall of the cave?

True, he said; how could they see anything but the shadows if they were never allowed to move their heads?

And of the objects which are being carried in like manner they would only see the shadows?

Yes, he said.

And if they were able to converse with one another, would they not suppose that they were naming what was actually before them?

Very true.

And suppose further that the prison had an echo which came from the other side, would they not be sure to fancy when one of the passers-by spoke that the voice which they heard came from the passing shadow?

No question, he replied.

To them, I said, the truth would be literally nothing but the shadows of the images.

That is certain.

And now look again, and see what will naturally follow if the prisoners are released and disabused of their error. At first, when any of them is liberated and compelled suddenly to stand up and turn his neck round and walk and look towards the light, he will suffer sharp pains; the glare will distress him, and he will be unable to see the realities of which in his former state he had seen the shadows; and then conceive some one saying to him, that what he saw before was an illusion, but that now, when he is approaching nearer to being and his eye is turned towards more real existence, he has a clearer vision—what will be his reply? And you may further imagine that his instructor is pointing to the objects as they pass and requiring him to name them—will he not be perplexed? Will he not fancy that the shadows which he formerly saw are truer than the objects which are now shown to him?

Far truer.

And if he is compelled to look straight at the light, will he not have a pain in his eyes which will make him turn away to take refuge in the objects of vision which he can see, and which he will conceive to be in reality clearer than the things which are now being shown to him?

True, he said.

And suppose once more, that he is reluctantly dragged up a steep and rugged ascent, and held fast until he is forced into the presence of the sun himself, is he not likely to be pained and irritated? When he approaches the light his eyes will be dazzled, and he will not be able to see anything at all of what are now called realities.

Not all in a moment, he said.

He will require to grow accustomed to the sight of the upper world. And first he will see the shadows best, next the reflections of men and other objects in the water, and then the objects themselves; then he will gaze upon the light of the moon and the stars and the spangled heaven; and he will see the sky and the stars by night better than the sun or the light of the sun by day?

Certainly.

Last of all he will be able to see the sun, and not mere reflections of him in the water, but he will see him in his own proper place, and not in another; and he will contemplate him as he is.

Certainly.

He will then proceed to argue that this is he who gives the season and the years, and is the guardian of all that is in the visible world, and in a certain way the cause of all things which he and his fellows have been accustomed to behold?

Clearly, he said, he would first see the sun and then reason about him.

And when he remembered his old habitation, and the wisdom of the den and his fellow-prisoners, do you not suppose that he would felicitate himself on the change, and pity them?

Certainly, he would.

And if they were in the habit of conferring honours among themselves on those who were quickest to observe the passing shadows and to remark which of them went before, and which followed after, and which were together; and who were therefore best able to draw conclusions as to the future, do you think that he would care for such honours and glories, or envy the possessors of them? Would he not say with Homer,

'Better to be the poor servant of a poor master,'

and to endure anything, rather than think as they do and live after their manner?

Yes, he said, I think that he would rather suffer anything than entertain these false notions and live in this miserable manner.

Imagine once more, I said, such a one coming suddenly out of the sun to be replaced in his old situation; would he not be certain to have his eyes full of darkness?

To be sure, he said.

And if there were a contest, and he had to compete in measuring the shadows with the prisoners who had never moved out of the den, while his sight was still weak, and before his eyes had become steady (and the time which would be needed to acquire this new habit of sight might be very considerable), would he not be ridiculous? Men would say of him that up he went and down he came without his eyes; and that it was better not even to think of ascending; and if any one tried to loose another and lead him up to the light, let them only catch the offender, and they would put him to death.

No question, he said.

This entire allegory, I said, you may now append, dear Glaucon, to the previous argument; the prison-house is the world of sight, the light of the fire is the sun, and you will not misapprehend me if you interpret the journey upwards to be the ascent of the soul into the intellectual world according to my poor belief, which, at your desire, I have expressed—whether rightly or wrongly God knows. But, whether true or false, my opinion is that in the world of knowledge the idea of good appears last of all, and is seen only with an effort; and, when seen, is also inferred to be the universal author of all things beautiful and right, parent of light and of the lord of light in this visible world, and the immediate source of reason and truth in the intellectual; and that this is the power upon which he who would act rationally either in public or private life must have his eye fixed.

ARISTOTLE, NICOMACHEAN ETHICS

INTRODUCTION

The ancient Greeks were different from us. At the core of their philosophies was the concept of *arête*. In its basic sense *arête* is 'excellence' of any kind. It means fulfilment of purpose or function – living up to one's full potential. This is a powerful starting point. It will be obvious that ancient Greek explorations of virtue, then, have something to offer those who seek an ethical path that goes beyond the bland amiability and do-goodism of our contemporary moral landscape.

Here's Aristotle's take on it.

Excellence is a product of nurture rather than of

nature. We acquire this excellence by literally *doing* acts that are virtuous: it is through doing acts of temperance that we become temperate and through doing acts of courage that we become courageous. In fact, 'acts of any kind produce habits or characters of the same kind', says Aristotle, and virtues and vices are no exception. Excellence is, at root, a kind of habit or character formed by relatively consistent actions of a related nature.

The correct method for cultivating excellence rests upon an appreciation of the effects of pleasure and pain. Excellence consists in finding pleasure in what is excellent and experiencing pain in what is mediocre. He who faces danger with pleasure (or at least without pain) is courageous; he to whom danger is painful is a coward. But pleasures and pains are not fixed; we find pleasure and pain largely as we have been taught. Man needs to be trained from his youth to find pleasure and pain in the right objects.

The ultimate goal of such cultivation is excellence, which means – for Aristotle as much as any ancient Greek – *arête* as the fulfilment of man's purpose or function. 'The proper excellence or virtue of man,' says Aristotle, 'will be the habit or trained faculty that makes him good and makes him perform his function well.' What makes a man good and perform his function well is to cultivate the habit of 'choosing the mean'. Courage stands at the mean between foolhardiness (in excess) and cowardice (in deficiency); pleasantness at the mean between buffoonery (in excess) and boorishness (in deficiency). But this 'mean' is to be understood in context. Fear, confidence, desire, anger, and pity may all stand at some distance from the mean in many contexts, but 'to be thus affected at the right times, and on the right occasions, and towards the right persons, and with the right object, and in the right fashion, is the mean course and the best course, and these are characteristics of virtue'.

This is a liberating philosophy and one of the highest manifestations of the rationality of the ancient Greek mind. Excellence is what makes us the best versions of ourselves; it is open to all as a product of such actions as are freely chosen; and it is a quality we can build up over time into what will come to constitute our basic character. It is a supremely optimistic as well as an ennobling philosophy for the modern man.

———————

BOOK II

I. MORAL VIRTUE IS ACQUIRED BY THE REPETITION OF THE CORRESPONDING ACTS

Excellence, then, being of these two kinds, intellectual and moral, intellectual excellence owes its birth and growth mainly to instruction, and so requires time and experience, while moral excellence is the result of habit or custom ('ethos'), and has accordingly in our language received a name formed by a slight change from 'ethos'.

From this it is plain that none of the moral excellences or virtues is implanted in us by nature; for that which is by nature cannot be altered by training. For instance, a stone naturally tends to fall downwards, and you could not train it to rise upwards, though you tried to do so by throwing it up ten thousand times, nor could you train fire to move downwards, nor accustom anything which naturally behaves in one way to behave in any other way.

The virtues, then, come neither by nature nor against nature, but nature gives the capacity for acquiring them, and this is developed by training.

Again, where we do things by nature we get the power first, and put this power forth in act afterwards: as we plainly see in the case of the senses; for it is not by constantly seeing and hearing that we acquire those faculties, but, on the contrary, we had the power first and then used it, instead of acquiring the power by the use. But the virtues we acquire by doing the acts, as is the case with the arts too. We learn an art by doing that which we wish to do when we have learned it; we become builders by building, and harpers by harping. And so by doing just acts we become just, and by doing acts of temperance and courage we become temperate and courageous.

This is attested, too, by what occurs in states; for the legislators make their citizens good by training;

i.e. this is the wish of all legislators, and those who do not succeed in this miss their aim, and it is this that distinguishes a good from a bad constitution.

Again, both the moral virtues and the corresponding vices result from and are formed by the same acts; and this is the case with the arts also. It is by harping that good harpers and bad harpers alike are produced: and so with builders and the rest; by building well they will become good builders, and bad builders by building badly. Indeed, if it were not so, they would not want anybody to teach them, but would all be born either good or bad at their trades. And it is just the same with the virtues also. It is by our conduct in our intercourse with other men that we become just or unjust, and by acting in circumstances of danger, and training ourselves to feel fear or confidence, that we become courageous or cowardly. So, too, with our animal appetites and the passion of anger; for by behaving in this way or in that on the occasions with which these passions are concerned, some become temperate and gentle, and others profligate and ill-tempered. In a word, acts of any kind produce habits or characters of the same kind.

Hence we ought to make sure that our acts be of a certain kind; for the resulting character varies as they vary. It makes no small difference, therefore, whether a man be trained from his youth up in this way or in that, but a great difference, or rather all the difference.

2. THESE ACTS MUST BE SUCH AS REASON PRESCRIBES; THEY CAN'T BE DEFINED EXACTLY, BUT MUST BE NEITHER TOO MUCH NOR TOO LITTLE

But our present inquiry has not, like the rest, a merely speculative aim; we are not inquiring merely in order to know what excellence or virtue is, but in order to become good; for otherwise it would profit us nothing. We must ask therefore about these acts, and see of what kind they are to be; for, as we said, it is they that determine our habits or character.

First of all, then, that they must be in accordance with right reason is a common characteristic of them, which we shall here take for granted, reserving for future discussion the question what this right reason is, and how it is related to the other excellences.

But let it be understood, before we go on, that all reasoning on matters of practice must be in outline merely, and not scientifically exact: for, as we said at starting, the kind of reasoning to be demanded varies with the subject in hand; and in practical matters and questions of expediency there are no invariable laws, any more than in questions of health.

And if our general conclusions are thus inexact, still more inexact is all reasoning about particular cases; for these fall under no system of scientifically established rules or traditional maxims, but the agent must always consider for himself what the special occasion requires, just as in medicine or navigation.

But though this is the case we must try to render what help we can.

First of all, then, we must observe that, in matters of this sort, to fall short and to exceed are alike fatal. This is plain (to illustrate what we cannot see by what we can see) in the case of strength and health. Too much and too little exercise alike destroy strength, and to take too much meat and drink, or to take too little, is equally ruinous to health, but the fitting amount produces and increases and preserves them. Just so, then, is it with temperance also, and courage, and the other virtues. The man who shuns and fears everything and never makes a stand, becomes a coward; while the man who fears nothing at all, but will face anything, becomes foolhardy. So, too, the man who takes his fill of any kind of pleasure, and abstains from none, is a profligate, but the man who shuns all (like him whom we call a 'boor') is devoid of sensibility. Thus temperance and courage are destroyed both by excess and defect, but preserved by moderation.

But habits or types of character are not only produced and preserved and destroyed by the same occasions and the same means, but they will also manifest themselves in the same circumstances. This is the case with palpable things like strength. Strength is produced by taking plenty of nourishment and doing plenty of hard work, and the strong man, in turn, has the greatest capacity for these. And the case is the same with the virtues: by abstaining from pleasure we become temperate, and when we have become temperate we are best able to abstain. And so with courage: by habituating ourselves to despise danger, and to face it, we become courageous; and when we have become courageous, we are best able to face danger.

3. VIRTUE IS IN VARIOUS WAYS CONCERNED WITH PLEASURE AND PAIN

The pleasure or pain that accompanies the acts must be taken as a test of the formed habit or character.

He who abstains from the pleasures of the body and rejoices in the abstinence is temperate, while he who is vexed at having to abstain is profligate; and again, he who faces danger with pleasure, or, at any rate, without pain, is courageous, but he to whom this is painful is a coward.

For moral virtue or excellence is closely concerned with pleasure and pain. It is pleasure that moves us to do what is base, and pain that moves us to refrain from what is noble. And therefore, as Plato says, man needs to be so trained from his youth up as to find pleasure and pain in the right objects. This is what sound education means.

Another reason why virtue has to do with pleasure and pain is that it has to do with actions and passions or affections; but every affection and every act is accompanied by pleasure or pain.

The fact is further attested by the employment of pleasure and pain in correction; they have a kind of curative property, and a cure is effected by administering the opposite of the disease.

Again, as we said before, every type of character is essentially relative to, and concerned with, those things that form it for good or for ill; but it is through pleasure and pain that bad characters are formed—that is to say, through pursuing and avoiding the wrong pleasures and pains, or pursuing and avoiding them at the wrong time, or in the wrong manner, or in any other of the various ways of going wrong that may be distinguished.

And hence some people go so far as to define the virtues as a kind of impassive or neutral state of mind. But they err in stating this absolutely, instead of qualifying it by the addition of the right and wrong manner, time, etc.

We may lay down, therefore, that this kind of excellence makes us do what is best in matters of pleasure and pain, while vice or badness has the contrary effect. But the following considerations will throw additional light on the point.

There are three kinds of things that move us to choose, and three that move us to avoid them: on the one hand, the beautiful or noble, the advantageous, the pleasant; on the other hand, the ugly or base, the hurtful, the painful. Now, the good man is apt to go right, and the bad man to go wrong, about them all, but especially about pleasure: for pleasure is not only common to man with animals, but also accompanies all pursuit or choice; since the noble, and the advantageous also, are pleasant in idea.

Again, the feeling of pleasure has been fostered in us all from our infancy by our training, and has thus become so engrained in our life that it can scarce be washed out. And, indeed, we all more or less make pleasure our test in judging of actions. For this reason too, then, our whole inquiry must be concerned with these matters; since to be pleased and pained in the right or the wrong way has great influence on our actions.

Again, to fight with pleasure is harder than to fight with wrath (which Heraclitus says is hard), and virtue, like art, is always more concerned with what is harder; for the harder the task the better is success. For this reason also, then, both virtue or excellence and the science of the state must always be concerned with pleasures and pains; for he that behaves rightly with regard to them will be good, and he that behaves badly will be bad.

We will take it as established, then, that excellence or virtue has to do with pleasures and pains; and that the acts which produce it develop it, and also, when differently done, destroy it; and that it manifests itself in the same acts which produced it.

...

6. VIZ., THE HABIT OF CHOOSING THE MEAN

We have thus found the genus to which virtue

belongs, but we want to know not only that it is a trained faculty, but also what species of trained faculty it is.

We may safely assert that the virtue or excellence of a thing causes that thing both to be itself in good condition and to perform its function well. The excellence of the eye, for instance, makes both the eye and its work good; for it is by the excellence of the eye that we see well. So the proper excellence of the horse makes a horse what he should be, and makes him good at running, and carrying his rider, and standing a charge.

If, then, this holds good in all cases, the proper excellence or virtue of man will be the habit or trained faculty that makes a man good and makes him perform his function well.

How this is to be done we have already said, but we may exhibit the same conclusion in another way, by inquiring what the nature of this virtue is.

Now, if we have any quantity, whether continuous or discrete, it is possible to take either a larger, or a smaller, or an equal amount, and that either absolutely or relatively to our own needs.

By an equal or fair amount I understand a mean amount, or one that lies between excess and deficiency.

By the absolute mean, or mean relatively to the thing itself, I understand that which is equidistant from both extremes, and this is one and the same for all.

By the mean relatively to us I understand that which is neither too much nor too little for us, and this is not one and the same for all.

For instance, if ten be larger and two be smaller, if we take six we take the mean relatively to the thing itself; for it exceeds one extreme by the same amount by which it is exceeded by the other extreme: and this is the mean in arithmetical proportion.

But the mean relatively to us cannot be found in this way. If ten pounds of food is too much for a given man to eat, and two pounds too little, it does not follow that the trainer will order him six pounds: for that also may perhaps be too much for the man in question, or too little; too little for Milo, too much for the beginner. The same holds true in running and wrestling.

And so we may say generally that a master in any art avoids what is too much and what is too little, and seeks for the mean and chooses it—not the absolute but the relative mean.

If, then, every art or science perfects its work in this way, looking to the mean and bringing its work up to this standard (so that people are wont to say of a good work that nothing could be taken from it or added to it, implying that excellence is destroyed by excess or deficiency, but secured by observing the mean; and good artists, as we say, do in fact keep their eyes fixed on this in all that they do), and if virtue, like nature, is more exact and better than any art, it follows that virtue also must aim at the mean—virtue of course meaning moral virtue or excellence; for it has to do with passions and actions, and it is these that admit of excess and deficiency and the mean. For instance, it is possible to feel fear, confidence, desire, anger, pity, and generally to be affected pleasantly and painfully, either too much or too little, in either case wrongly; but to be thus affected at the right times, and on the right occasions, and towards the right persons, and with the right object, and in the right fashion, is the mean course and the best course, and these are characteristics of virtue. And in the same way, our outward acts also admit of excess and deficiency, and the mean or due amount.

Virtue, then, has to deal with feelings or passions and with outward acts, in which excess is wrong and deficiency also is blamed, but the mean amount is praised and is right—both of which are characteristics of virtue.

Virtue, then, is a kind of moderation, inasmuch as it aims at the mean or moderate amount.

Again, there are many ways of going wrong (for evil is infinite in nature, to use a Pythagorean figure, while good is finite), but only one way of going right; so that the one is easy and the other hard—easy to miss the mark and hard to hit. On this account also, then, excess and deficiency are characteristic of vice, hitting the mean is characteristic of virtue:

'*Goodness is simple, ill takes any shape.*'

Virtue, then, is a habit or trained faculty of choice, the characteristic of which lies in moderation or observance of the mean relatively to the persons concerned, as determined by reason, i.e. by the reason by which the prudent man would determine it. And it is a moderation, firstly, inasmuch as it comes in the middle or mean between two vices, one on the side of excess, the other on the side of defect; and, secondly, inasmuch as, while these vices fall short of or exceed the due measure in feeling and in action, it finds and chooses the mean, middling, or moderate amount.

Regarded in its essence, therefore, or according to the definition of its nature, virtue is a moderation or middle state, but viewed in its relation to what is best and right it is the extreme of perfection.

But it is not all actions nor all passions that admit of moderation; there are some whose very names imply badness, as malevolence, shamelessness, envy, and, among acts, adultery, theft, murder. These and all other like things are blamed as being bad in themselves, and not merely in their excess or deficiency. It is impossible therefore to go right in them; they are always wrong: rightness and wrongness in such things (e.g. in adultery) does not depend upon whether it is the right person and occasion and manner, but the mere doing of any one of them is wrong.

It would be equally absurd to look for moderation or excess or deficiency in unjust cowardly or profligate conduct; for then there would be moderation in excess or deficiency, and excess in excess, and deficiency in deficiency.

The fact is that just as there can be no excess or deficiency in temperance or courage because the mean or moderate amount is, in a sense, an extreme, so in these kinds of conduct also there can be no moderation or excess or deficiency, but the acts are wrong however they be done. For, to put it generally, there cannot be moderation in excess or deficiency, nor excess or deficiency in moderation.

...

9. THE MEAN HARD TO HIT, AND IS A MATTER OF PERCEPTION, NOT OF REASONING

We have sufficiently explained, then, that moral virtue is moderation or observance of the mean, and in what sense, viz. (1) as holding a middle position between two vices, one on the side of excess, and the other on the side of deficiency, and (2) as aiming at the mean or moderate amount both in feeling and in action.

And on this account it is a hard thing to be good; for finding the middle or the mean in each case is a hard thing, just as finding the middle or centre of a circle is a thing that is not within the power of everybody, but only of him who has the requisite knowledge.

Thus anyone can be angry—that is quite easy; anyone can give money away or spend it: but to do these things to the right person, to the right extent, at the right time, with the right object, and in the right manner, is not what everybody can do, and is by no means easy; and that is the reason why right doing is rare and praiseworthy and noble.

He that aims at the mean, then, should first of all strive to avoid that extreme which is more opposed to it, as Calypso bids Ulysses—

'Clear of these smoking breakers keep thy ship.'

For of the extremes, one is more dangerous, the other less. Since then it is hard to hit the mean precisely, we must 'row when we cannot sail', as the proverb has it, and choose the least of two evils; and that will be best effected in the way we have described.

And secondly we must consider, each for himself, what we are most prone to—for different natures are inclined to different things—which we may learn by the pleasure or pain we feel. And then we must bend ourselves in the opposite direction; for by keeping well away from error we shall fall into the middle course, as we straighten a bent stick by bending it the other way.

But in all cases we must be especially on our guard against pleasant things, and against pleasure; for we can scarce judge her impartially. And so, in our behaviour towards her, we should imitate the behaviour of the old counsellors towards Helen, and in all cases repeat their saying: if we dismiss her we shall be less likely to go wrong.

But it is a hard task, we must admit, especially in a particular case. It is not easy to determine, for instance, how and with whom one ought to be angry, and upon what grounds, and for how long; for public opinion sometimes praises those who fall short, and calls them gentle, and sometimes applies the term manly to those who show a harsh temper.

In fact, a slight error, whether on the side of excess or deficiency, is not blamed, but only a considerable error; for then there can be no mistake. But it is hardly possible to determine by reasoning how far or to what extent a man must err in order to incur blame, and indeed matters that fall within the scope of perception never can be so determined. Such matters lie within the region of particulars, and can only be determined by perception.

So much then is plain, that the middle character is in all cases to be praised, but that we ought to incline sometimes towards excess, sometimes towards deficiency; for in this way we shall most easily hit the mean and attain to right doing.

3

MARCUS AURELIUS, MEDITATIONS

INTRODUCTION

Philosopher, soldier, emperor – Marcus Aurelius Antoninus Augustus, better known as simply 'Marcus Aurelius', was all of these and more. Plato had once dreamed of a philosopher king. In Marcus Aurelius, the classical world finally had one.

We could write at length on the enlightened nature of his imperial rule – his support for orphans and the poor, his interest in manumission (freeing) of slaves, and his tolerance for free speech. We could also write at length of his military campaigns and triumphs – his victory in the East as co-ruler with his adopted brother Verus against the Parthians, invading from what is modern-day Iran, as well as his defence against marauding Germans swarming into Roman territory from across the Danube in the north. On any basis, it is no surprise that he was considered the last of the five 'good emperors'.

What is really of interest, though, is the philosophy that underpinned these achievements.

Marcus Aurelius was a Stoic. The rational man, according to the Stoics, takes active and positive command of his emotions. Desire, fear, and even pain arise from false judgments: nothing affects us unless we choose to let it. Only those who can grasp these truths are truly free. All others are slaves.

The *Meditations* are a high point of Stoic thinking, but they are also one of a kind. Marcus Aurelius left us more than merely a philosophy. What he left was a code of conduct for dealing with the stresses and strains endured as ruler of one of the greatest empires known to man. Large portions of the work appear to have been composed when the emperor was on campaign in the Roman province of Pannonia, near modern-day Austria and Hungary – a land of gloomy forest, gigantic oaks, and birds with feathers that 'shine like fires at night'. It was there, at the edge of his empire and surrounded by ferocious barbarian tribes, that Marcus Aurelius gave birth to the writings that have inspired leaders and thinkers for centuries. It's no surprise that these reflections are rooted in practical concerns and form the bedrock of a practical ethos.

How, then, to live?

Accept. Begin every day with this simple reminder: today I shall meet with the busybody, the ungrateful, the arrogant, the deceitful, the envious, the antisocial. They are this way through their own ignorance of what is good and what is evil. No matter: nothing they say or do can have any effect on me. They cannot implicate me in what is ugly, what angry, or what is hateful unless I am complicit in this. Work with them. To act against one another is contrary to nature.

Take control. Dig deep. Retreat inside yourself. Go to the place where nothing can touch your soul. From there you will find that what disturbs you now disturbs you as a result of your own judgment about it – and it is in your power to wipe out this judgment now. Such as a man's habitual thoughts are, such is the character of his mind. Where a man can live he can live well. To do that, keep the contents of the mind clean, and correct, and self-composed.

Focus on the present. Don't spend time thinking of the whole course of one's life. Don't allow your thoughts to roam over potential troubles that may befall you in a hypothetical future. At all times consider what it is in the present moment that pains or is intolerable to you. You will find this circle of the present to be a very circumscribed one. Loss is nothing else than change, and change – like all things – gives pleasure or pain just as our judgment would render it.

This is a noble philosophy not because it comes

from an emperor but because it reflects a nobility of spirit. Here is nothing servile: the whole basis of the philosophy is the rediscovery of our native freedom. Here is nothing needy: all that is required is to take command of oneself and one's reactions. And here is nothing small: a good disposition towards our fellow men is invincible if genuine. Go out and live as a man aware of his true nature, says Marcus Aurelius, and you will do well enough.

BOOK II

1. Begin the morning by saying to yourself, I shall meet with the busybody, the ungrateful, arrogant, deceitful, envious, unsocial. All these things happen to them by reason of their ignorance of what is good and evil. But I who have seen the nature of the good that it is beautiful, and of the bad that it is ugly, and the nature of him who does wrong, that it is akin to me; not only of the same blood or seed, but that it participates in the same intelligence and the same portion of the divinity, I can neither be injured by any of them, for no one can fix on me what is ugly, nor can I be angry with my kinsman, nor hate him. For we are made for cooperation, like feet, like hands, like eyelids, like the rows of the upper and lower teeth. To act against one another, then, is contrary to nature;

and it is acting against one another to be vexed and to turn away.

5. Every moment think steadily as a Roman and a man to do what you have in hand with perfect and simple dignity, and feeling of affection, and freedom, and justice, and to give yourself relief from all other thoughts. And you will give yourself relief if you do every act of your life as if it were the last, laying aside all carelessness and passionate aversion from the commands of reason, and all hypocrisy, and self-love, and discontent with the portion which has been given to you. You see how few the things are, the which if a man lays hold of, he is able to live a life which flows in quiet, and is like the existence of the gods; for the gods on their part will require nothing more from him who observes these things.

16. The soul of man does violence to itself, first of all, when it becomes an abscess, and, as it were, a tumour on the universe, so far as it can. For to be vexed at anything which happens is a separation of ourselves from nature, in some part of which the natures of all other things are contained. In the next place, the soul does violence to itself when it turns away from any man, or even moves towards him with the intention of injuring, such as are the souls of those who are angry. In the third place, the soul does violence to itself when it is overpowered by pleasure or by pain. Fourthly, when it plays a part, and does or says anything insincerely and untruly. Fifthly, when it allows any act of its own and any movement to be

without an aim, and does anything thoughtlessly and without considering what it is, it being right that even the smallest things be done with reference to an end; and the end of rational animals is to follow the reason and the law of the most ancient city and polity.

BOOK IV

3. Men seek retreats for themselves, houses in the country, seashores, and mountains; and you too are wont to desire such things very much. But this is altogether a mark of the most common sort of men, for it is in your power whenever you shall choose to retire into yourself. For nowhere either with more quiet or more freedom from trouble does a man retire than into his own soul, particularly when he has within him such thoughts that by looking into them he is immediately in perfect tranquility; and I affirm that tranquility is nothing else than the good ordering of the mind. Constantly then give to yourself this retreat, and renew yourself; and let your principles be brief and fundamental, which, as soon as you shall recur to them, will be sufficient to cleanse the soul completely, and to send you back free from all discontent with the things to which you return. For with what are you discontented? With the badness of men? Recall to your mind this conclusion, that rational animals exist for one another, and that to endure is a part of justice, and that men do wrong

involuntarily; and consider how many already, after mutual enmity, suspicion, hatred, and fighting, have been stretched dead, reduced to ashes; and be quiet at last. But perhaps you are dissatisfied with that which is assigned to you out of the universe. Recall to your recollection this alternative; either there is providence or atoms; or remember the arguments by which it has been proved that the world is a kind of political community. But perhaps corporeal things will still fasten upon you. Consider then further that the mind mingles not with the breath, whether moving gently or violently, when it has once drawn itself apart and discovered its own power, and think also of all that you have heard and assented to about pain and pleasure. But perhaps the desire of the thing called fame will torment you. See how soon everything is forgotten, and look at the chaos of infinite time on each side of the present, and the emptiness of applause, and the changeableness and want of judgment in those who pretend to give praise, and the narrowness of the space within which it is circumscribed. For the whole earth is a point, and how small a nook in it is this your dwelling, and how few are there in it, and what kind of people are they who will praise you.

This then remains: Remember to retire into this little territory of your own, and above all do not distract or strain yourself, but be free, and look at things as a man, as a human being, as a citizen, as a mortal. But among the things ready to thy hand to which you shall turn, let there be these, which are two. One is that things do not touch the soul, for they are external and remain immovable; but our perturbations come only from the opinion which is within. The other is that all these things, which you see, change immediately and will no longer be; and constantly bear in mind how many of these changes you have already witnessed. The universe is transformation; life is opinion.

7. Take away your opinion, and then there is taken away the complaint, 'I have been harmed'. Take away the complaint, 'I have been harmed', and the harm is taken away.

36. Observe constantly that all things take place by change, and accustom yourself to consider that the nature of the Universe loves nothing so much as to change the things which are and to make new things like them. For everything that exists is in a manner the seed of that which will be. But you are thinking only of seeds which are cast into the earth or into a womb: but this is a very vulgar notion.

39. What is evil to you does not subsist in the ruling principle of another; nor yet in any turning and mutation of your corporeal covering. Where is it then? It is in that part of you in which subsists the power of forming opinions about evils. Let this power then not form such opinions, and all is well. And if that which is nearest to it, the poor body, is cut, burnt, filled with matter and rottenness, nevertheless let the part which forms opinions about these things

be quiet; that is, let it judge that nothing is either bad or good which can happen equally to the bad man and the good. For that which happens equally to him who lives contrary to nature and to him who lives according to nature, is neither according to nature nor contrary to nature.

40. Constantly regard the universe as one living being, having one substance and one soul; and observe how all things have reference to one perception, the perception of this one living being; and how all things act with one movement; and how all things are the cooperating causes of all things which exist; observe too the continuous spinning of the thread and the contexture of the web.

BOOK V

16. Such as are your habitual thoughts, such also will be the character of your mind; for the soul is dyed by the thoughts. Dye it then with a continuous series of such thoughts as these: for instance, that where a man can live, there he can also live well. But he must live in a palace; well then, he can also live well in a palace. And again, consider that for whatever purpose each thing has been constituted, for this it has been constituted, and towards this it is carried; and its end is in that towards which it is carried; and where the end is, there also is the advantage and the good of each thing. Now the good for the reasonable

animal is society; for that we are made for society has been shown above. Is it not plain that the inferior exists for the sake of the superior? But the things which have life are superior to those which have not life, and of those which have life the superior are those which have reason.

19. Things themselves touch not the soul, not in the least degree; nor have they admission to the soul, nor can they turn or move the soul: but the soul turns and moves itself alone, and whatever judgments it may think proper to make, such it makes for itself the things which present themselves to it.

20. In one respect man is the nearest thing to me, so far as I must do good to men and endure them. But so far as some men make themselves obstacles to my proper acts, man becomes to me one of the things which are indifferent, no less than the sun or wind or a wild beast. Now it is true that these may impede my action, but they are no impediments to my affects and disposition, which have the power of acting conditionally and changing: for the mind converts and changes every hindrance to its activity into an aid; and so that which is a hindrance is made a furtherance to an act; and that which is an obstacle on the road helps us on this road.

26. Let the part of your soul which leads and governs be undisturbed by the movements in the flesh, whether of pleasure or of pain; and let it not unite with them, but let it circumscribe itself and limit those affects to their parts. But when these

affects rise up to the mind by virtue of that other sympathy that naturally exists in a body which is all one, then you must not strive to resist the sensation, for it is natural: but let not the ruling part of itself add to the sensation the opinion that it is either good or bad.

BOOK VI

6. The best way of avenging yourself is not to become like the wrongdoer.

19. If a thing is difficult to be accomplished by yourself, do not think that it is impossible for man: but if anything is possible for man and conformable to his nature, think that this can be attained by yourself too.

20. In the gymnastic exercises suppose that a man has torn you with his nails, and by dashing against your head has inflicted a wound. Well, we neither show any signs of vexation, nor are we offended, nor do we suspect him afterwards as a treacherous fellow; and yet we are on our guard against him, not however as an enemy, nor yet with suspicion, but we quietly get out of his way. Something like this let thy behaviour be in all the other parts of life; let us overlook many things in those who are like antagonists in the gymnasium. For it is in our power, as I said, to get out of the way, and to have no suspicion nor hatred.

BOOK VII

2. How can our principles become dead, unless the impressions which correspond to them are extinguished? But it is in your power continuously to fan these thoughts into a flame. I can have that opinion about anything which I ought to have. If I can, why am I disturbed? The things which are external to my mind have no relation at all to my mind. Let this be the state of your affects, and you stand erect. To recover your life is in your power. Look at things again as you used to look at them; for in this consists the recovery of your life.

29. Wipe out the imagination. Stop the pulling of the strings. Confine yourself to the present. Understand well what happens either to you or to another. Divide and distribute every object into the causal and the material. Think of your last hour. Let the wrong which is done by a man stay there where the wrong was done.

64. In every pain let this thought be present, that there is no dishonour in it, nor does it make the governing intelligence worse, for it does not damage the intelligence either so far as the intelligence is rational or so far as it is social. Indeed in the case of most pains let this remark of Epicurus aid you, that pain is neither intolerable nor everlasting, if you bear in mind that it has its limits, and if you add nothing to it in imagination: and remember this too, that we do not perceive that many things which are disagreeable

to us are the same as pain, such as excessive drowsiness, and the being scorched by heat, and the having no appetite. When then you are about any of these things, say to yourself that you are yielding to pain.

BOOK VIII

36. Do not disturb yourself by thinking of the whole of your life. Let not your thoughts at once embrace all the various troubles which you may expect to befall you; but on every occasion ask yourself, 'What is there in this which is intolerable and past bearing?', for you will be ashamed to confess. In the next place remember that neither the future nor the past pains you, but only the present. But this is reduced to a very little, if you only circumscribe it, and chide your mind if it is unable to hold out against even this.

47. If you are pained by any external thing, it is not this thing that disturbs you, but your own judgment about it. And it is in your power to wipe out this judgment now. But if anything in your own disposition gives you pain, who hinders you from correcting your opinion? And even if you are pained because you are not doing some particular thing which seems to you to be right, why do you not rather act than complain? But some insuperable obstacle is in the way? Do not be grieved then, for the cause of its not being done depends not on you. But it is not

worth while to live if this cannot be done. Take your departure then from life contentedly, just as he dies who is in full activity, and well pleased too with the things which are obstacles.

49. Say nothing more to yourself than what the first appearances report. Suppose that it has been reported to you that a certain person speaks ill of you. This has been reported; but that you have been injured, that has not been reported. I see that my child is sick. I do see; but that he is in danger, I do not see. Thus then always abide by the first appearances, and add nothing yourself from within, and then nothing happens to you. Or rather add something like a man who knows everything that happens in the world.

50. A cucumber is bitter – throw it away. There are briars in the road – turn aside from them. This is enough. Do not add: And why were such things made in the world? For you will be ridiculed by a man who is acquainted with nature, as you would be ridiculed by a carpenter and shoemaker if you did find fault because you see in their workshop shavings and cuttings from the things which they make. And yet they have places into which they can throw these shavings and cuttings, and the universal nature has no external space; but the wondrous part of her art is that though she has circumscribed herself, everything within her which appears to decay and to grow old and to be useless she changes into herself, and again makes other new things from these very same, so that she requires neither substance from without nor

wants a place into which she may cast that which decays. She is content then with her own space, and her own matter, and her own art.

BOOK IX

30. Look down from above on the countless herds of men and their countless solemnities, and the infinitely varied voyagings in storms and calms, and the differences among those who are born, who live together, and die. And consider, too, the life lived by others in olden time, and the life of those who will live after thee, and the life now lived among barbarous nations, and how many know not even your name, and how many will soon forget it, and how they who perhaps now are praising you will very soon blame you, and that neither a posthumous name is of any value, nor reputation, nor anything else.

35. Loss is nothing else than change. But the universal nature delights in change, and in obedience to her all things are now done well, and from eternity have been in like form, and will be such to time without end. What, then, do you say – that all things have been and all things always will be bad, and that no power has ever been found in so many gods to rectify these things, but the world has been condemned to be bound in never ceasing evil?

42. When you are offended with any man's shameless conduct, immediately ask yourself, 'Is it

possible, then, that shameless men should not be in the world?' It is not possible. Do not, then, require what is impossible. For this man also is one of those shameless men who must of necessity be in the world. Let the same considerations be present to your mind in the case of the knave, and the faithless man, and of every man who does wrong in any way. For at the same time that you do remind yourself that it is impossible that such kind of men should not exist, you will become more kindly disposed towards every one individually. It is useful to perceive this, too, immediately when the occasion arises, what virtue nature has given to man to oppose to every wrongful act. For she has given to man, as an antidote against the stupid man, mildness, and against another kind of man some other power. And in all cases it is possible for you to correct by teaching the man who is gone astray; for every man who errs misses his object and is gone astray. Besides, wherein have you been injured? For you will find that no one among those against whom you are irritated has done anything by which your mind could be made worse; but that which is evil to you and harmful has its foundation only in the mind. And what harm is done or what is there strange, if the man who has not been instructed does the acts of an uninstructed man? Consider whether you should not rather blame yourself because you did not expect such a man to err in such a way. For you had means given you by your reason to suppose that it was likely that he would commit this error, and yet you have forgotten and are amazed that he has erred. But most of all when you blame a man as faithless or ungrateful, turn to yourself. For the fault is manifestly your own, whether you did trust that a man who had such a disposition would keep his promise, or when conferring your kindness you did not confer it absolutely, nor yet in such way as to have received from your very act all the profit. For what more do you want when you have done a man a service? Are you not content that you have done something conformable to your nature, and do you seek to be paid for it? Just as if the eye demanded a recompense for seeing, or the feet for walking. For as these members are formed for a particular purpose, and by working according to their several constitutions obtain what is their own; so also as man is formed by nature to acts of benevolence, when he has done anything benevolent or in any other way conducive to the common interest, he has acted conformably to his constitution, and he gets what is his own.

BOOK XI

18. If any have offended against you, consider first: what is my relation to men, and that we are made for one another; and in another respect I was made to be set over them, as a ram over the flock or a bull over the herd. But examine the matter from first principles, from this. If all things are not mere atoms, it is nature

which orders all things: if this is so, the inferior things exist for the sake of the superior, and these for the sake of one another.

Second, consider what kind of men they are at table, in bed, and so forth; and particularly, under what compulsions in respect of opinions they are; and as to their acts, consider with what pride they do what they do.

Third, that if men do rightly what they do, we ought not to be displeased: but if they do not right, it is plain that they do so involuntarily and in ignorance. For as every soul is unwillingly deprived of the truth, so also is it unwillingly deprived of the power of behaving to each man according to his deserts. Accordingly, men are pained when they are called unjust, ungrateful, and greedy, and in a word wrongdoers to their neighbours.

Fourth, consider that you also do many things wrong, and that you are a man like others; and even if you do abstain from certain faults, still you have the disposition to commit them, though either through cowardice, or concern about reputation, or some such mean motive, you do abstain from such faults.

Fifth, consider that you do not even understand whether men are doing wrong or not, for many things are done with a certain reference to circumstances. And in short, a man must learn a great deal to enable him to pass a correct judgment on another man's acts.

Sixth, consider when you are much vexed or

grieved, that man's life is only a moment, and after a short time we are all laid out dead.

Seventh, that it is not men's acts which disturb us, for those acts have their foundation in men's ruling principles, but it is our own opinions which disturb us. Take away these opinions then, and resolve to dismiss your judgment about an act as if it were something grievous, and your anger is gone. How then shall I take away these opinions? By reflecting that no wrongful act of another brings shame on you: for unless that which is shameful is alone bad, you also must of necessity do many things wrong, and become a robber and everything else.

Eighth, consider how much more pain is brought on us by the anger and vexation caused by such acts than by the acts themselves, at which we are angry and vexed.

Ninth, consider that a good disposition is invincible if it be genuine, and not an affected smile and acting a part. For what will the most violent man do to you, if you continue to be of a kind disposition towards him, and if, as opportunity offers, you gently admonish him and calmly correct his errors at the very time when he is trying to do you harm, saying, 'Not so, my child: we are constituted by nature for something else; I shall certainly not be injured, but you are injuring yourself, my child.' And show him with gentle tact and by general principles that this is so, and that even bees do not do as he does, nor any animals which are formed by nature to be gregarious.

And you must do this neither with any double meaning nor in the way of reproach, but affectionately and without any rancour in your soul; and not as if you were lecturing him, nor yet that any bystander may admire, but either when he is alone, and if others are present.

Remember these nine rules, as if you had received them as a gift from the Muses, and begin at last to be a man while you live. But you must equally avoid nattering men and being vexed at them, for both are unsocial and lead to harm. And let this truth be present to you in the excitement of anger, that to be moved by passion is not manly, but that mildness and gentleness, as they are more agreeable to human nature, so also are they more manly; and he who possesses these qualities possesses strength, nerves, and courage, and not the man who is subject to fits of passion and discontent. For in the same degree in which a man's mind is nearer to freedom from all passion, in the same degree also is it nearer to strength; and as the sense of pain is a characteristic of weakness, so also is anger. For he who yields to pain and he who yields to anger, both are wounded and both submit.

But if you will, receive also a tenth present from the leader of the Muses, Apollo, and it is this – that to expect bad men not to do wrong is madness, for he who expects this desires an impossibility. But to allow men to behave so to others, and to expect them not to do you any wrong, is irrational and tyrannical.

CHUANG-TZU, THE WRITINGS OF CHUANG-TZU

INTRODUCTION

If a man dreams he is a butterfly and then awakes, what is he? The answer seems simple: he is a man who has dreamt he is a butterfly. Take a step back, though – look at it from the perspective of the dream – and it's not so clear. In the dream the total consciousness was of being a butterfly; there was no consciousness of being a man. Now, out of the dream, there is total consciousness of being a man, and no consciousness of being a butterfly. The priority of one over the other only appears from the perspective of impressions received at the current moment. How does the man know, then, whether he was a man dreaming he was a butterfly – or is now a butterfly dreaming he is a man?

The *Writings* of Chuang-tzu – the second masterpiece of Daoist philosophy after the *Tao Te Ching* – is comprised of many provocative short pieces in the vein of 'Dreaming of a Butterfly'. This collection of anecdotes, fables, allegories, and parables has been traditionally attributed to Chuang-tzu (also known as Zhuang Zhou and Zhuangzi), a Chinese sage who lived around the fourth century BC in the Warring States period. The details of Chuang-tzu's life have now faded into obscurity. But that doesn't matter. The writings that bear his name speak across the millennia as if barely a day had passed between them and us.

What is it, though, of which they speak?

They speak first and foremost of the 'Dao' – the cosmic 'Way' that flows through and unites all things. The Dao is the nameless organising principle within all existence that defies conceptualization and changes spontaneously according to its own inner nature. It is all-encompassing and as fully present in emptiness as it is in fullness. To live in accordance with the Dao is to bring one's own limited being into harmony with this immense force.

They speak of human wrongheadedness in the face of the Dao. We cut ourselves off from the spontaneity of existence through over-analysis and need for control. We take for absolute truth what is, in reality, nothing more than a partial, limited, and temporary perspective. We resist change rather than accept that change is a creator every bit as a much as it is a destroyer.

And they speak, ultimately, of a better way of living. For Chuang-tzu that meant 'wuwei'. *Wuwei* is 'actionless action'. It is action beyond activity – action without busy-ness, action without striving, action without friction or reactivity. *Wuwei* implies a calm appreciation for paths of least resistance and the real likelihood that doing nothing is the best choice. Just as the expert cook never attempts to chop through bones or joints but instead slides his blade through the openings and cavities that are naturally present in the animal, so the man skilled in living finds his course through life.

CHAPTER 2

DREAMING OF A BUTTERFLY

Once upon a time, I, Chuang Tzŭ, dreamt I was a butterfly, fluttering hither and thither, to all intents and purposes a butterfly. I was conscious only of following my fancies as a butterfly, and was unconscious of my individuality as a man. Suddenly, I awoke, and there I lay, myself again. Now I do not know whether I was then a man dreaming I was a butterfly, or whether I am now a butterfly dreaming

I am a man. Between a man and a butterfly there is necessarily a barrier. The transition is called *Metempsychosis*.

CHAPTER 3

COOK DING CUTS UP AN OX

My life has a limit, but my knowledge is without limit. To drive the limited in search of the limitless is fatal, and the knowledge of those who do this is fatally lost.

In striving for others, avoid fame. In striving for self, avoid disgrace. Pursue a middle course. Thus you will keep a sound body, and a sound mind, fulfil your duties, and work out your allotted span.

Prince Hui's cook was cutting up a bullock. Every blow of his hand, every heave of his shoulders, every tread of his foot, every thrust of his knee, every *whshh* of rent flesh, every *chhk* of the chopper, was in perfect harmony – rhythmical like the dance of the Mulberry Grove, simultaneous like the chords of the Ching Shou.

'Well done!' cried the Prince. 'Yours is skill indeed.'

'Sire,' replied the cook, 'I have always devoted myself to Tao. It is better than skill. When I first began to cut up bullocks, I saw before me simply *whole* bullocks. After three years' practice, I saw no more whole animals. And now I work with my mind and not with my eye. When my senses bid me stop, but my mind urges me on, I fall back upon eternal principles. I follow such openings or cavities as there may be, according to the natural constitution of the animal. I do not attempt to cut through joints; still less through large bones.

'A good cook changes his chopper once a year – because he cuts. An ordinary cook, once a month – because he hacks. But I have had this chopper nineteen years, and although I have cut up many thousand bullocks, its edge is as if fresh from the whetstone. For at the joints there are always interstices, and the edge of a chopper being without thickness, it remains only to insert that which is without thickness into such an interstice. By these means, the interstice will be enlarged, and the blade will find plenty of room. It is thus that I have kept my chopper for nineteen years as though fresh from the whetstone.

'Nevertheless, when I come upon a hard part where the blade meets with a difficulty, I am all caution. I fix my eye on it. I stay my hand, and gently apply my blade, until with a *hwah* the part yields like earth crumbling to the ground. Then I take out my chopper, and stand up, and look around, and pause, until with an air of triumph I wipe my chopper and put it carefully away.'

'Bravo!' cried the Prince. 'From the words of this cook I have learnt how to take care of my life.'

CHAPTER 4

A USELESS TREE

A certain artisan was travelling to the Ch'i State. On reaching Ch'ü-yüan, he saw a sacred *li* tree, large enough to hide an ox behind it, a hundred spans in girth, towering up ten cubits over the hill top, and carrying behind it branches, many tens of the smallest of which were of a size for boats. Crowds stood gazing at it, but our artisan took no notice, and went on his way without even casting a look behind. His apprentice, however, gazed his fill, and when he caught up his master, said, 'Ever since I have handled an adze in your service, I have never seen such a splendid piece of timber as that. How was it that you, sir, did not care to stop and look at it?'

'It's not worth talking about,' replied his master. 'It's good for nothing. Make a boat of it – 'twould sink. A coffin – 'twould rot. Furniture – 'twould soon break down. A door – 'twould sweat. A pillar – 'twould be worm-eaten. It is wood of no quality, and of no use. That is why it has attained its present age.'

When the artisan reached home, he dreamt that the tree appeared to him in a dream and spoke as follows: 'What is it that you compare me with? Is it with the more elegant trees? The cherry-apple, the pear, the orange, the pomelo, and other fruit-bearers, as soon as their fruit ripens are stripped and treated with indignity. The great boughs are snapped off, the small ones scattered abroad. Thus do these trees by their own value injure their own lives. They cannot fulfil their allotted span of years, but perish prematurely in mid-career from their entanglement with the world around them. Thus it is with all things. For a long period, my aim was to be useless. Many times I was in danger, but at length I succeeded, and so became useful as I am today. But had I then been of use, I should not now be of the great use I am. Moreover, you and I belong both to the same category of things. Have done then with this criticism of others. Is a good-for-nothing fellow whose dangers are not yet passed a fit person to talk of a good-for-nothing tree?'

When our artisan awoke and told his dream, his apprentice said, 'If the tree aimed at uselessness, how was it that it became a sacred tree?'

'What you don't understand,' replied his master, 'don't talk about. That was merely to escape from the attacks of its enemies. Had it not become sacred, how many would have wanted to cut it down! The means of safety adopted were different from ordinary means, and to test these by ordinary canons leaves one far wide of the mark.'

Tzŭ Ch'i of Nan-poh was travelling on the Shang mountain when he saw a large tree which astonished him very much. A thousand chariot teams could have found shelter under its shade.

'What tree is this?' cried Tzŭ Ch'i. 'Surely it must have unusually fine timber.' Then looking up, he saw that its branches were too crooked for rafters; while as to the trunk he saw that its irregular grain made it valueless for coffins. He tasted a leaf, but it took the skin off his lips, and its odour was so strong that it would make a man as it were drunk for three days together.

'Ah!' said Tzŭ Ch'i. 'This tree is good for nothing, and that is how it has attained this size. A wise man might well follow its example.'

CHAPTER 17

UNIVERSAL ENVY

The walrus envies the centipede; the centipede envies the snake; the snake envies the wind; the wind envies the eye; the eye envies the mind.

The walrus said to the centipede, 'I hop about on one leg, but not very successfully. How do you manage all these legs you have?'

'I don't manage them,' replied the centipede. 'Have you never seen saliva? When it is ejected, the big drops are the size of pearls, the small ones like mist. They fall promiscuously on the ground and cannot be counted. And so it is that my mechanism works naturally, without my being conscious of the fact.'

The centipede said to the snake, 'With all my legs I do not move as fast as you with none. How is that?'

'One's natural mechanism,' replied the snake, 'is not a thing to be changed. What need have I for legs?'

The snake said to the wind, 'I can manage to wriggle along, but I have a form. Now you come blustering down from the north sea to bluster away to the south sea, and you seem to be without form. How is that?'

"Tis true,' replied the wind, 'that I bluster as you say; but anyone who can point at me or kick at me, excels me. On the other hand, I can break huge trees and destroy large buildings. That is my strong point. Out of all the small things in which I do not excel I make one great one in which I do excel. And to excel in great things is given only to the Sages.'

CHAPTER 17

THE DEBATE ON THE JOY OF FISH

Chuang Tzŭ and Hui Tzŭ had strolled on to the bridge over the Hao, when the former observed, 'See how the minnows are darting about! That is the pleasure of fishes.'

'You not being a fish yourself,' said Hui Tzŭ, 'how can you possibly know in what consists the pleasure of fishes?'

'And you not being I,' retorted Chuang Tzŭ, 'how can you know that I do not know?'

'If I, not being you, cannot know what you know,'

urged Hui Tzŭ, 'it follows that you, not being a fish, cannot know in what consists the pleasure of fishes.'

'Let us go back,' said Chuang Tzŭ, 'to your original question. You asked me how I knew in what consists the pleasure of fishes. Your very question shows that you knew I knew. I knew it from my own feelings on this bridge.'

CHAPTER 18

DRUMMING ON A TUB AND SINGING

When Chuang Tzŭ's wife died, Hui Tzŭ went to condole. He found the widower sitting on the ground, singing, with his legs spread out at a right angle, and beating time on a bowl.

'To live with your wife,' exclaimed Hui Tzŭ, 'and see your eldest son grow up to be a man, and then not to shed a tear over her corpse – this would be bad enough. But to drum on a bowl, and sing; surely this is going too far.'

'Not at all,' replied Chuang Tzŭ. 'When she died, I could not help being affected by her death. Soon, however, I remembered that she had already existed in a previous state before birth, without form, or even substance; that while in that unconditioned condition, substance was added to spirit; that this substance then assumed form; and that the next stage was birth. And now, by virtue of a further change, she is dead, passing from one phase to another like the sequence of spring, summer, autumn, and winter. And while she is thus lying asleep in Eternity, for me to go about weeping and wailing would be to proclaim myself ignorant of these natural laws. Therefore I refrain.'

CHAPTER 20

EMPTY BOATS

'Suppose a boat is crossing a river, and another empty boat is about to collide with it. Even an irritable man would not lose his temper. But supposing there was someone in the second boat. Then the occupant of the first would shout to him to keep clear. And if the other did not hear the first time, nor even when called to three times, bad language would inevitably follow. In the first case there was no anger, in the second there was; because in the first case the boat was empty, and in the second it was occupied. And so it is with man. If he could only roam empty through life, who would be able to injure him?'

5

NICCOLÒ MACHIAVELLI, THE PRINCE

INTRODUCTION

All those who achieve and retain power have a little bit of Machiavelli about them.

Machiavelli is now best known as a proponent of the dark arts of statecraft. In his guidebook for rulers, *The Prince*, Machiavelli insisted on the employment of all means necessary to protect the state and the prince's position within it, explaining that to act entirely in accordance with one's professions of virtue would be self-defeating because the world is so full of evil that anyone doing so would soon be destroyed. This was a philosophy that, despite being widely applied in practice, would receive little sympathy or appreciation in Christian Europe. The Catholic Church banned *The Prince*, putting it on the Index Librorum Prohibitorum – the list of forbidden books.

At the heart of Machiavelli's approach is his realism. We could talk of an imaginary world, he suggests, where rulers display all the virtues and studiously abstain from vices. But that would be pointless. Better to face up to the fact that none can be possessed of, nor display, all the virtues. Instead, the ruler's job is to avoid the reproach of those vices that would cause the loss of his state. As to those vices that would not cause harm to the state – well, says Machiavelli, those should be avoided, if possible. But, in the real world, there is also a third category of vices – those that positively assist the ruler in maintaining his state. Reproach for these vices need not cause the ruler unease: sometimes what looks like virtue will bring ruin, while what looks like vice will bring security and prosperity.

A good example of Machiavelli's approach can be seen in his discussion of the virtue of 'liberality' and the corresponding vice of 'meanness'. Machiavelli does not approach these in theological or abstract moral terms. Instead, he looks at their relevance for governing the state. The problem with liberality, says Machiavelli, is that it wastes rapidly: as you exercise liberality, you begin – through your own expenditure – to lose the very power to do so. The ruler finding himself short of funds, as a result, must face two consequences: he will be hated as he weighs down upon and taxes his people, and he will be despised for being poor. There are, however, two circumstances when the general rule does not apply. You can spend freely when you are on your way to becoming ruler because at that stage you need to buy support. You can also spend freely when you spend money belonging to citizens of other states, whether obtained through extortion or pillage. In the first case, liberality is necessary in order to obtain the state in the first place; in the second case, the resentment of the expropriated citizens of other states will pose no threat.

Is it better for a ruler to be loved or feared? Machiavelli admits that, in theory, it would be better to be both loved *and* feared. In reality, though, the ruler will often need to make a choice. Given that this is so, the better choice is to be feared. Men are, in general, contemptible creatures. When you are successful they will offer blood, property, life, and children in your support. But when you need their help they turn against you. Fear, on the other hand, has a more prolonged effect: it protects and preserves you by a dread of punishment that never fails. It is crucial, though, never to be hated, which means, in particular, abstaining from the subjects' property – and their women.

Ultimately, the ruler needs to combine aspects of both the fox and the lion. The world does not operate exclusively by law; it operates also by force. For that reason, the ruler must cultivate within himself something of the animal. But why the fox and why the lion? It is necessary to be a fox to discover the snares, says Machiavelli, and it is necessary to be a lion to terrify the wolves. Cunning and ferociousness must each be applied at the right times against the right targets.

What is Machiavelli's relevance to the modern man?

In answer to this, it is illuminating to have regard to the viewpoint of the Italian philosopher, Antonio Gramsci. Gramsci took the view that Machiavelli did not write *The Prince* for the benefit of the ruling classes – they already knew what the art of statecraft involved and how these principles should be applied. In fact, thought Gramsci, Machiavelli was writing for the *next* generation of rulers, as it was these who would need to learn the true nature of statecraft. If that is correct, then *The Prince* is a guide not for use by the establishment against the people. It is, instead, a guide for the ordinary man as he steps ever forward towards reclaiming his sovereignty.

It is a guide for everyman.

A guide, reader, for you.

———

CHAPTER 15

CONCERNING THINGS FOR WHICH MEN, AND
ESPECIALLY PRINCES, ARE PRAISED OR BLAMED

It remains now to see what ought to be the rules of conduct for a prince towards subject and friends. And as I know that many have written on this point, I expect I shall be considered presumptuous in mentioning it again, especially as in discussing it I shall depart from the methods of other people. But, it being my intention to write a thing which shall be useful to him who apprehends it, it appears to me more appropriate to follow up the real truth of the matter than the imagination of it; for many have pictured republics and principalities which in fact have never been known or seen, because how one lives is so far distant from how one ought to live, that he who neglects what is done for what ought to be done, sooner effects his ruin than his preservation; for a man who wishes to act entirely up to his professions of virtue soon meets with what destroys him among so much that is evil.

Hence it is necessary for a prince wishing to hold his own to know how to do wrong, and to make use of it or not according to necessity. Therefore, putting on one side imaginary things concerning a prince, and discussing those which are real, I say that all men when they are spoken of, and chiefly princes for being more highly placed, are remarkable for some of those qualities which bring them either blame or praise; and thus it is that one is reputed liberal, another miserly, using a Tuscan term (because an avaricious person in our language is still he who desires to possess by robbery, whilst we call one miserly who deprives himself too much of the use of his own); one is reputed generous, one rapacious; one cruel, one compassionate; one faithless, another faithful; one effeminate and cowardly, another bold and brave; one affable, another haughty; one lascivious, another chaste; one sincere, another cunning; one hard, another easy; one grave, another frivolous; one religious, another unbelieving, and the like. And I know that everyone will confess that it would be most praiseworthy in a prince to exhibit all the above qualities that are considered good; but because they can neither be entirely possessed nor observed, for human conditions do not permit it, it is necessary for him to be sufficiently prudent that he may know how to avoid the reproach of those vices which would lose him his state; and also to keep himself, if it be possible, from those which would not lose him it; but this not being possible, he may with less hesitation abandon himself to them. And again, he need not make himself uneasy at incurring a reproach for those vices without which the state can only be saved with difficulty, for if everything is considered carefully, it will be found that something which looks like virtue, if followed, would be his ruin; whilst something else,

which looks like vice, yet followed brings him security
and prosperity.

CHAPTER 16

CONCERNING LIBERALITY AND MEANNESS

Commencing then with the first of the above-named
characteristics, I say that it would be well to be
reputed liberal. Nevertheless, liberality exercised in
a way that does not bring you the reputation for it,
injures you; for if one exercises it honestly and as it
should be exercised, it may not become known, and
you will not avoid the reproach of its opposite.
Therefore, anyone wishing to maintain among men
the name of liberal is obliged to avoid no attribute
of magnificence; so that a prince thus inclined will
consume in such acts all his property, and will be
compelled in the end, if he wish to maintain the name
of liberal, to unduly weigh down his people, and tax
them, and do everything he can to get money. This
will soon make him odious to his subjects, and
becoming poor he will be little valued by any one;
thus, with his liberality, having offended many and
rewarded few, he is affected by the very first trouble
and imperilled by whatever may be the first danger;
recognizing this himself, and wishing to draw back
from it, he runs at once into the reproach of being
miserly.

Therefore, a prince, not being able to exercise this virtue of liberality in such a way that it is recognized, except to his cost, if he is wise he ought not to fear the reputation of being mean, for in time he will come to be more considered than if liberal, seeing that with his economy his revenues are enough, that he can defend himself against all attacks, and is able to engage in enterprises without burdening his people; thus it comes to pass that he exercises liberality towards all from whom he does not take, who are numberless, and meanness towards those to whom he does not give, who are few.

We have not seen great things done in our time except by those who have been considered mean; the rest have failed. Pope Julius the Second was assisted in reaching the papacy by a reputation for liberality, yet he did not strive afterwards to keep it up, when he made war on the King of France; and he made many wars without imposing any extraordinary tax on his subjects, for he supplied his additional expenses out of his long thriftiness. The present King of Spain would not have undertaken or conquered in so many enterprises if he had been reputed liberal. A prince, therefore, provided that he has not to rob his subjects, that he can defend himself, that he does not become poor and abject, that he is not forced to become rapacious, ought to hold of little account a reputation for being mean, for it is one of those vices which will enable him to govern.

And if any one should say: Caesar obtained empire

by liberality, and many others have reached the highest positions by having been liberal, and by being considered so, I answer: Either you are a prince in fact, or in a way to become one. In the first case, this liberality is dangerous, in the second it is very necessary to be considered liberal; and Caesar was one of those who wished to become pre-eminent in Rome; but if he had survived after becoming so, and had not moderated his expenses, he would have destroyed his government. And if any one should reply: Many have been princes, and have done great things with armies, who have been considered very liberal, I reply: Either a prince spends that which is his own or his subjects' or else that of others. In the first case he ought to be sparing, in the second he ought not to neglect any opportunity for liberality. And to the prince who goes forth with his army, supporting it by pillage, sack, and extortion, handling that which belongs to others, this liberality is necessary, otherwise he would not be followed by soldiers. And of that which is neither yours nor your subjects' you can be a ready giver, as were Cyrus, Caesar, and Alexander; because it does not take away your reputation if you squander that of others, but adds to it; it is only squandering your own that injures you.

And there is nothing wastes so rapidly as liberality, for even whilst you exercise it you lose the power to do so, and so become either poor or despised, or else, in avoiding poverty, rapacious and hated. And a prince should guard himself, above all things, against being despised and hated; and liberality leads you to both. Therefore it is wiser to have a reputation for meanness which brings reproach without hatred than to be compelled through seeking a reputation for liberality to incur a name for rapacity which begets reproach with hatred.

CHAPTER 17

CONCERNING CRUELTY AND CLEMENCY, AND WHETHER IT IS BETTER TO BE LOVED THAN FEARED

Coming now to the other qualities mentioned above, I say that every prince ought to desire to be considered clement and not cruel. Nevertheless, he ought to take care not to misuse this clemency. Cesare Borgia was considered cruel; notwithstanding, his cruelty reconciled the Romagna, unified it, and restored it to peace and loyalty. And if this be rightly considered, he will be seen to have been much more merciful than the Florentine people, who, to avoid a reputation for cruelty, permitted Pistoia to be destroyed. Therefore a prince, so long as he keeps his subjects united and loyal, ought not to mind the reproach of cruelty; because with a few examples he will be more merciful than those who, through too much mercy, allow disorders to arise, from which follow murders or robberies; for these are wont to injure the whole people, whilst those executions which originate with a prince offend the individual only.

And of all princes, it is impossible for the new prince to avoid the imputation of cruelty, owing to new states being full of dangers. Hence Virgil, through the mouth of Dido, excuses the inhumanity of her reign owing to its being new, saying:

'*Res dura, et regni novitas me talia cogunt*
Moliri, et late fines custode tueri.'

['. . . *against my will, my fate*
A throne unsettled, and an infant state,
Bid me defend my realms with all my pow'rs,
And guard with these severities my shores.]

Nevertheless, he ought to be slow to believe and to act, nor should he himself show fear, but proceed in a temperate manner with prudence and humanity, so that too much confidence may not make him incautious and too much distrust render him intolerable.

Upon this, a question arises: whether it be better to be loved than feared or feared than loved? It may be answered that one should wish to be both, but, because it is difficult to unite them in one person, it is much safer to be feared than loved, when, of the two, either must be dispensed with. Because this is to be asserted in general of men, that they are ungrateful, fickle, false, cowardly, covetous, and as long as you succeed they are yours entirely; they will offer you their blood, property, life, and children, as is said above, when the need is far distant; but when it approaches they turn against you. And that prince who, relying entirely on their promises, has neglected other precautions, is ruined; because friendships that are obtained by payments, and not by greatness or nobility of mind, may indeed be earned, but they are not secured, and in time of need cannot be relied upon; and men have less scruple in offending one who is beloved than one who is feared, for love is preserved by the link of obligation which, owing to the baseness of men, is broken at every opportunity for their advantage; but fear preserves you by a dread of punishment which never fails.

Nevertheless, a prince ought to inspire fear in such a way that, if he does not win love, he avoids hatred; because he can endure very well being feared whilst he is not hated, which will always be as long as he abstains from the property of his citizens and subjects and from their women. But when it is necessary for him to proceed against the life of someone, he must do it on proper justification and for manifest cause, but above all things he must keep his hands off the property of others, because men more quickly forget the death of their father than the loss of their patrimony. Besides, pretexts for taking away the property are never wanting; for he who has once begun to live by robbery will always find pretexts for seizing what belongs to others; but reasons for taking life, on the contrary, are more difficult to find and sooner lapse. But when a prince is with his army, and has under control a multitude of soldiers, then it is quite necessary for him to disregard the reputation of cruelty, for without it he would never hold his army united or disposed to its duties.

Among the wonderful deeds of Hannibal this one is enumerated: that having led an enormous army, composed of many various races of men, to fight in foreign lands, no dissensions arose either among them or against the prince, whether in his bad or in his good fortune. This arose from nothing else than his inhuman cruelty, which, with his boundless valour, made him revered and terrible in the sight of his soldiers, but without that cruelty, his other virtues were not sufficient to produce this effect. And shortsighted writers admire his deeds from one point of view and from another condemn the principal cause of them. That it is true his other virtues would not have been sufficient for him may be proved by the case of Scipio, that most excellent man, not only of his own times but within the memory of man, against whom, nevertheless, his army rebelled in Spain; this arose from nothing but his too great forbearance, which gave his soldiers more license than is consistent with military discipline. For this, he was upbraided in the Senate by Fabius Maximus, and called the corrupter of the Roman soldiery. The Locrians were laid waste by a legate of Scipio, yet they were not avenged by him, nor was the insolence of the legate punished, owing entirely to his easy nature. Insomuch that someone in the Senate, wishing to excuse him, said there were many men who knew much better how not to err than to correct the errors of others. This disposition, if he had been continued in the command, would have destroyed in time the fame and glory of Scipio; but, he being under the control of the Senate, this injurious characteristic not only concealed itself but contributed to his glory.

Returning to the question of being feared or loved, I come to the conclusion that men loving according to their own will and fearing according to that of the prince, a wise prince should establish himself on that which is in his own control and not in that of others; he must endeavour only to avoid hatred, as is noted.

CHAPTER 18

CONCERNING THE WAY IN WHICH PRINCES SHOULD KEEP FAITH

Every one admits how praiseworthy it is in a prince to keep faith, and to live with integrity and not with craft. Nevertheless our experience has been that those princes who have done great things have held good faith of little account, and have known how to circumvent the intellect of men by craft, and in the end have overcome those who have relied on their word. You must know there are two ways of contesting, the one by the law, the other by force; the first method is proper to men, the second to beasts; but because the first is frequently not sufficient, it is necessary to have recourse to the second. Therefore it is necessary for a prince to understand how to avail himself of the beast and the man. This has been figuratively taught to princes by ancient writers, who describe how Achilles and many other princes of old were given to the Centaur Chiron to nurse, who brought them up in his discipline; which means solely that, as they had for a teacher one who was half beast and half man, so it is necessary for a prince to know how to make use of both natures, and that one without the other is not durable. A prince, therefore, being compelled knowingly to adopt the beast, ought to choose the fox and the lion; because the lion cannot defend himself against snares and the fox cannot defend himself against wolves. Therefore, it is necessary to be a fox to discover the snares and a lion to terrify the wolves. Those who rely simply on the lion do not understand what they are about. Therefore a wise lord cannot, nor ought he to, keep faith when such observance may be turned against him, and when the reasons that caused him to pledge it exist no longer. If men were entirely good this precept would not hold, but because they are bad, and will not keep faith with you, you too are not bound to observe it with them. Nor will there ever be wanting to a prince legitimate reasons to excuse this non-observance. Of this endless modern examples could be given, showing how many treaties and engagements have been made void and of no effect through the faithlessness of princes; and he who has known best how to employ the fox has succeeded best.

But it is necessary to know well how to disguise this characteristic, and to be a great pretender and dissembler; and men are so simple, and so subject to present necessities, that he who seeks to deceive will always find someone who will allow himself to be deceived. One recent example I cannot pass over in silence. Alexander the Sixth did nothing else but deceive men, nor ever thought of doing otherwise, and he always found victims; for there never was a man who had greater power in asserting, or who with greater oaths would affirm a thing, yet would observe it less; nevertheless his deceits always succeeded according to his wishes, because he well understood this side of mankind.

Therefore it is unnecessary for a prince to have all the good qualities I have enumerated, but it is very necessary to appear to have them. And I shall dare to say this also, that to have them and always to observe them is injurious, and that to appear to have them is useful; to appear merciful, faithful, humane, religious, upright, and to be so, but with a mind so framed that should you require not to be so, you may be able and know how to change to the opposite.

And you have to understand this, that a prince, especially a new one, cannot observe all those things for which men are esteemed, being often forced, in order to maintain the state, to act contrary to fidelity, friendship, humanity, and religion. Therefore it is necessary for him to have a mind ready to turn itself accordingly as the winds and variations of fortune force it, yet, as I have said above, not to diverge from the good if he can avoid doing so, but, if compelled, then to know how to set about it.

For this reason, a prince ought to take care that he never lets anything slip from his lips that is not replete with the above-named five qualities, that he may appear to him who sees and hears him altogether merciful, faithful, humane, upright, and religious. There is nothing more necessary to appear to have than this last quality, inasmuch as men judge generally more by the eye than by the hand, because it belongs to everybody to see you, to few to come in touch with you. Everyone sees what you appear to be, few really know what you are, and those few dare not oppose themselves to the opinion of the many, who have the majesty of the state to defend them; and in the actions of all men, and especially of princes, which it is not prudent to challenge, one judges by the result.

For that reason, let a prince have the credit of conquering and holding his state, the means will always be considered honest, and he will be praised by everybody; because the vulgar are always taken by what a thing seems to be and by what comes of it; and in the world there are only the vulgar, for the few find a place there only when the many have no ground to rest on.

One prince[1] of the present time, whom it is not well to name, never preaches anything else but peace and good faith, and to both he is most hostile, and either, if he had kept it, would have deprived him of reputation and kingdom many a time.

---

1. Ferdinand of Aragon.

6

BALDASSARE CASTIGLIONE, THE COURTIER

INTRODUCTION

One of the more striking aspects of twenty-first-century life is our almost universal (although often unacknowledged) tolerance for personal limitation. We want our athletes to be athletes, our scholars to be scholars, our soldiers to be soldiers, and our lawyers to be lawyers. For a man to cultivate himself in multiple fields is seen as eccentric and aberrant. We don't know what to do with, and don't much welcome, lawyer-athletes or scholar-soldiers. We are not much interested in the balanced development of the whole man.

It wasn't always like this.

Our Renaissance forebears, in particular, wanted to cultivate a different kind of human being.

Preeminent among those who attempted to define this ideal man was Baldassare Castiglione. Castiglione was himself a courtier, diplomat, soldier, and author. As a young man, he had taken up residence in the court of Urbino – the most refined and elegant of the Italian courts – where he learned the ways of the Renaissance courtier. The memory of that period stayed with him and formed the basis of the book that he would publish in the year before his death, *The Courtier*.

The Courtier asks a simple but important question: What makes the ideal man?

Castiglione's answer describes what has come to be known as 'Renaissance man'. He needs to be accomplished – in sports, conversation, poetry, music, drawing, and dancing. He needs to be able to speak gracefully and appropriately with people from all stations in life. He should know the classics and write well without slavishly imitating others. He should be respectful of the surrounding customs and more humble than his own station in life requires. He has to be able to earn the respect of his peers. Interestingly, though, he doesn't need to be of noble birth, because nobility can be learned by reference to the best examples of it in life and in history.

Above all, he must display what Castiglione refers to as *sprezzatura*. *Sprezzatura* is the fundamental characteristic of true civility. It is a kind of grace –

'a certain nonchalance' showing that what is done is done without effort and almost without thought. It is the skill of making something difficult look easy and thereby demonstrating the real skill of the performer. It would be a misunderstanding, however, to consider that *sprezzatura* can be achieved by *artificial* nonchalance, for that is still effortful and therefore ungraceful. True *sprezzatura* is achieved when athleticism, wit, and artistry are so deeply realised in the core of your being that they are already aspects of yourself.

The Courtier has the twin virtues of being able both to expand our horizons and to focus our vision. It expands us by pointing to the need for a return to the idea of a man as balanced and cultivated whole rather than an attenuated technical labour unit. And it focuses our thoughts upon the elemental quality of this fully developed man: the incorporation of his skills into the core of his being so that they can be carried out with civility and grace.

It is the perfect counterpoise to the pressures of our age.

BOOK ONE

24. 'If I remember rightly, Sir Count, I think you have repeated several times this evening that the Courtier must accompany his actions, gestures, habits, in short

his every movement, with grace; and this you seem to regard as a universal seasoning, without which all other properties and good qualities are of little worth. And indeed I think that in this everyone would allow himself to be persuaded easily, since from the very force of the word, it may be said that he who has grace finds grace. But since you said that this is oftentimes the gift of nature and of heaven and, even when not thus perfect, can with care and pains be made much greater – those men who are born so fortunate and so rich in this treasure as are some we see, seem to me in this to have little need of other master, because that benign favour of heaven almost in spite of themselves leads them higher than they will, and makes them not only pleasing but admirable to all the world. Therefore I do not discuss this, it not being in our power to acquire it of ourselves. But they who have received from nature only so much, that they are capable of becoming graceful by pains, industry, and care – I long to know by what art, by what training, by what method, they can acquire this grace, as well in bodily exercises (in which you esteem it to be so necessary) as also in everything else that they may do or say. Therefore, since by much praise of this quality you have aroused in all of us, I think, an ardent thirst to pursue it, you are further bound, by the charge that my lady Emilia laid upon you, to satisfy that thirst by teaching us how to attain it.'

25. 'I am not bound,' said the Count, 'to teach you how to become graceful, or anything else; but only

to show you what manner of man a perfect Courtier ought to be. Nor would I in any case undertake the task of teaching you this perfection; especially having said a little while ago that the Courtier must know how to wrestle, vault, and do many other things, which I am sure you all know quite as well as if I, who have never learned them, were to teach you. For just as a good soldier knows how to tell the smith what fashion, shape and quality his armour ought to have, but cannot show how it is to be made or forged or tempered; so I perhaps may be able to tell you what manner of man a perfect Courtier ought to be, but cannot teach you what you must do to become one.

'Yet to comply with your request as far as is within my power – although it is almost a proverb that grace is not to be learned – I say that whoever would acquire grace in bodily exercises (assuming first that he be by nature not incapable), ought to begin early and learn the rudiments from the best masters. And how important this seemed to King Philip of Macedon may be seen from the fact that he chose Aristotle, the famous philosopher and perhaps the greatest that has ever been in the world, to teach his son Alexander the first elements of letters. And of the men whom we know at the present day, consider how well and how gracefully my lord Galeazzo Sanseverino, the Grand Equerry of France, performs all bodily exercises; and this because in addition to the natural aptitude of person that he possesses, he has taken the utmost pains to study with good masters, and always to have about him men who excel and to select from each the best of what they know: for just as in wrestling, vaulting and in the use of many sorts of weapons, he has taken for his guide our friend Messer Pietro Monte, who (as you know) is the true and only master of every form of trained strength and agility, so in riding, jousting and all else, he has ever had before his eyes the most proficient men that were known in those matters.

26. 'Therefore he who wishes to be a good pupil, besides performing his tasks well, must put forth every effort to resemble his master, and, if it were possible, to transform himself into his master. And when he feels that he has made some progress, it will be very profitable to observe different men of the same calling, and governing himself with that good judgment which must ever be his guide, to go about selecting now this thing from one and that thing from another. And as the bee in the green meadows is ever wont to rob the flowers among the grass, so our Courtier must steal this grace from all who seem to possess it, taking from each that part which shall most be worthy praise; and not act like a friend of ours whom you all know, who thought he greatly resembled King Ferdinand the Younger of Aragon, and made it his care to imitate the latter in nothing but a certain trick of continually raising the head and twisting one side of the mouth, which the king had contracted from some infirmity. And there are many such, who think they gain a point if only they be like

a great man in something; and frequently they devote themselves to that which is his only fault.

'But having before now often considered whence this grace springs, laying aside those men who have it by nature, I find one universal rule concerning it, which seems to me worth more in this matter than any other in all things human that are done or said: and that is to avoid affectation to the uttermost and as it were a very sharp and dangerous rock; and, to use possibly a new word, to practise in everything a certain nonchalance that shall conceal design and show that what is done and said is done without effort and almost without thought. From this I believe grace is in large measure derived, because everyone knows the difficulty of those things that are rare and well done, and therefore facility in them excites the highest admiration; while on the other hand, to strive and as the saying is to drag by the hair, is extremely ungraceful, and makes us esteem everything slightly, however great it be.

'Accordingly, we may affirm that to be true art which does not appear to be art; nor to anything must we give greater care than to conceal art, for if it is discovered it quite destroys our credit and brings us into small esteem. And I remember having once read that there were several very excellent orators of antiquity, who among their other devices strove to make everyone believe that they had no knowledge of letters; and hiding their knowledge they pretended that their orations were composed very simply and as if springing rather from nature and truth than from study and art; the which, if it had been detected, would have made men wary of being duped by it.

'Thus you see how the exhibition of art and study so intense destroys the grace in everything. Which of you is there who does not laugh when our friend Messer Pierpaolo dances in his peculiar way, with those capers of his legs stiff to the toe and head motionless, as if he were a stick, and with such intentness that he actually seems to be counting the steps? What eye so blind as not to see in this the ungracefulness of affectation, and in many men and women who are here present, the grace of that nonchalant ease (for in the case of bodily movements many call it thus), showing by word or laugh or gesture that they have no care and are thinking more of everything else than of that, to make the onlooker think they can hardly go amiss?'

27. Messer Bernardo Bibbiena here said, without waiting:

'Now, at last, our friend Messer Roberto has found someone to praise the manner of his dancing, as all the rest of you seem to value it lightly; because if this merit consists in nonchalance, and in appearing to take no heed and to be thinking more of everything else than of what you are doing, Messer Roberto in dancing has no peer on earth; for to show plainly that he is not thinking about it, he often lets the cloak drop from his shoulders and the slippers from his feet, and still goes on dancing without picking up either the one or the other.'

Then the Count replied:

'Since you insist on my talking, I will speak further of our faults. Do you not perceive that what you call nonchalance in Messer Roberto, is really affectation? For it is clearly seen that he is striving with all his might to seem to be taking no thought, and this is taking too much thought; and since it passes the true limits of moderation, his nonchalance is affected and unbecoming; and it is a thing that works precisely the reverse of the effect intended, that is the concealment of art. Thus in nonchalance (which is praiseworthy in itself), I do not think that it is less a vice of affectation to let the clothes fall from one's back, than in care of dress (which also is praiseworthy in itself) to hold the head stiff for fear of disarranging one's locks, or to carry a mirror in the peak of one's cap and a comb in one's sleeve, and to have a valet follow one about the streets with sponge and brush: for such care in dress and such nonchalance both touch upon excess, which is always offensive and contrary to that pure and charming simplicity which is so pleasing to the human mind.

'You see how ungraceful a rider is who strives to sit bolt upright in the saddle after the manner we are wont to call Venetian, as compared with another who seems not to be thinking about it, and sits his horse as free and steady as if he were afoot. How much more pleasing and how much more praised is a gentleman who carries arms, if he be modest, speak little and boast little, than another who is forever sounding his own praises, and with blasphemy and bluster seems to be hurling defiance at the world! This too is naught but affectation of wishing to appear bold. And so it is with every exercise, nay with everything that can be done or said in the world.'

28. Then my lord Magnifico said:

'This is true also with music, wherein it is a very great fault to place two perfect consonances one after the other, so that our very sense of hearing abhors it and often enjoys a second or seventh, which in itself is a harsh and intolerable discord. And the reason is that repetition of perfect consonances begets satiety and exhibits a too affected harmony; which is avoided by introducing imperfect consonances, and thus a kind of contrast is given, whereby our ears are held more in suspense, and more eagerly await and enjoy the perfect consonances, and sometimes delight in that discord of the second or seventh, as in something unpremeditated.'

'You see then,' replied the Count, 'the harmful effect of affectation in this as in other things. It is said also to have been proverbial among some very excellent painters of antiquity, that over diligence is harmful, and Protogenes is said to have been censured by Apelles because he did not know when to take his hand from the tablet.

Then Messer Cesare said:

'Methinks our friend Fra Serafino has this same

fault, of not knowing when to take his hands from the table, at least until all the food has been taken from it too.'

The Count laughed, and continued:

'Apelles meant that in his painting Protogenes did not know when he had finished, which was the same thing as reproving him for being affected in his work. Thus this excellence, which is the opposite of affectation and which for the present we call nonchalance, besides being the true fountain from which grace springs, carries with it another ornament, which, in accompanying any human action whatever and however trifling it be, not only at once reveals the knowledge of him who performs it, but often leads us to rate his knowledge as much greater than in fact it is because it impresses upon the minds of the bystanders the idea that he who does well so easily, knows much more than he does, and that if he were to use care and effort in what he did, he could do it far better.

'And to multiply like examples, here is a man who handles weapons, either about to throw a dart or holding a sword in his hand or other weapon; if he nimbly and without thinking puts himself in an attitude of readiness, with such ease that his body and all his members seem to fall into that posture naturally and quite without effort – although he do no more, he will prove himself to everyone to be perfect in that exercise. Likewise in dancing, a single step, a single movement of the person that is graceful and not forced, soon shows the knowledge of the dancer. A musician who in singing utters a single note ending with sweet tone in a little group of four notes with such ease as to seem spontaneous, shows by that single touch that he can do much more than he is doing. Often too in painting, a single line not laboured, a single brush-stroke easily drawn, so that it seems as if the hand moves unbidden to its aim according to the painter's wish, without being guided by care or any skill, clearly reveals the excellence of the craftsman, which every man appreciates according to his capacity for judging. And the same is true of nearly everything else.'

7

BALTASAR GRACIÁN, THE ART OF WORLDLY WISDOM

INTRODUCTION

There is no better guide to living and advancing in the world than Baltasar Gracián's *The Art of Worldly Wisdom*.

Gracián is a truth-teller and a real-talker. There is no feel-good tomfoolery here. He provides precise and pithy instruction on how to live in world of rogues and charlatans – and guidance for the man who wishes to survive and prosper in that world without becoming rogue or charlatan himself.

The book – a collection of 300 maxims – has been

of enduring appeal. It was 'especially fitted to be the manual of those who live in the great world,' said Schopenhauer. 'To read it once through is obviously not enough; it is a book made for constant use as occasion serves – in short, to be a companion for life.' Nietzsche was equally impressed. 'Europe has never produced anything finer or more complicated in matters of moral subtlety,' he thought. Churchill is said to have read it on the ship taking him to the Boer Wars. The most recent editions have sold in hundreds of thousands and in multiple languages.

What, then, is the source of its appeal?

Gracián's foundation stone is his candour. He looks at the world straight and tells us how he sees it without asking or expecting it to be anything other than it actually is – a play of appearances. 'Things do not pass for what they are but for what they seem,' he says. Most people are deceived by appearances and only see what is shown to them.

In this environment, the prudent man neither relies wholly on his own intrinsic virtue and good deeds nor does he turn to superficiality and deception. What he does instead is to both *be* of use and at the same time *show* himself to be of use – to close the gap between appearance and reality rather than disregarding either one of them.

The essential quality needed in order to negotiate this complex and dangerous world is self-possession. There is no higher rule than that over oneself and over one's impulses, says Gracián. It means never to be put out even by the most adverse circumstances. It also means: don't talk about yourself or parade your position; speak well of rivals and detractors; and don't be importunate or overeager to please. It is characteristic of Gracián that he does not advocate this self-possession on a theological or moral basis. He advocates it for the fundamental reason that it brings benefit. For it is this kind of self-restraint, says Gracián, that displays a man's superiority and advances him in the world.

Having established his self-possession, the wise man then accommodates himself to the social world in which he finds himself. Adapt yourself to the moods of those around you, says Gracián. Think with the few and speak with the many. Adopt the fashions of the present rather than those of the past. Don't on your own condemn what all others approve. And don't hold your views too firmly: you may be wrong, and – even if you are not wrong – your willingness to consider alternative views will be taken by others as a courtesy, and will serve you well.

Ultimately, The Art of Worldly Wisdom communicates a certain way of seeing the world. Man, says Gracián, is a fundamentally social creature. Outside society, he is little more than an animal and deserves to be treated like one. There is nothing wrong in taking the social approach by checking one's own passions and prejudices. Quite the contrary. It is the mark of the civilised, sophisticated, and superior man to do so.

SELECTED MAXIMS

1. EVERYTHING IS AT ITS ACME;

especially the art of making one's way in the world. There is more required nowadays to make a single wise man than formerly to make Seven Sages, and more is needed nowadays to deal with a single person than was required with a whole people in former time.

2. CHARACTER AND INTELLECT:

the two poles of our capacity; one without the other is but halfway to happiness. Intellect sufficeth not, character is also needed. On the other hand, it is the fool's misfortune to fail in obtaining the position, the employment, the neighbourhood, and the circle of friends that suit him.

3. KEEP MATTERS FOR A TIME IN SUSPENSE.

Admiration at their novelty heightens the value of your achievements. It is both useless and insipid to play with the cards on the table. If you do not declare yourself immediately, you arouse expectation, especially when the importance of your position makes you the object of general attention. Mix a little mystery with everything, and the very mystery arouses veneration. And when you explain, be not too explicit, just as you do not expose your inmost thoughts in ordinary intercourse. Cautious silence is the holy of holies of worldly wisdom. A resolution declared is never highly thought of; it only leaves room for criticism. And if it happens to fail, you are doubly unfortunate. Besides, you imitate the Divine way when you cause men to wonder and watch.

5. CREATE A FEELING OF DEPENDENCE.

Not he that adorns but he that adores makes a divinity. The wise man would rather see men needing him than thanking him. To keep them on the threshold of hope is diplomatic, to trust to their gratitude boorish; hope has a good memory, gratitude a bad one. More is to be got from dependence than from courtesy. He that has satisfied his thirst turns his back on the well, and the orange once sucked falls from the golden platter into the wastebasket. When dependence disappears, good behaviour goes with it as well as respect. Let it be one of the chief lessons of experience to keep hope alive without entirely satisfying it, by preserving it to make oneself always needed even by a patron on the throne. But let not silence be carried to excess lest you go wrong, nor let another's failing grow incurable for the sake of your own advantage.

7. AVOID VICTORIES OVER SUPERIORS.

All victories breed hate, and that over your superior is foolish or fatal. Superiority is always detested, *a fortiori* superiority over superiority. Caution can gloss over common advantages; for example, good looks may be cloaked by careless attire. There be some that will grant you precedence in good luck or good temper, but none in good sense, least of all a prince; for good sense is a royal prerogative, any claim to that is a case of lèse majesté. They are princes, and wish to be so in that most princely of qualities. They will allow a man to help them but not to surpass them, and will have any advice tendered them appear like a recollection of something they have forgotten rather than as a guide to something they cannot find. The stars teach us this finesse with happy tact; though they are his children and brilliant like him, they never rival the brilliancy of the sun.

8. TO BE WITHOUT PASSIONS.

'Tis a privilege of the highest order of mind. Their very eminence redeems them from being affected by transient and low impulses. There is no higher rule than that over oneself, over one's impulses: there is the triumph of free will. While passion rules the character, no aiming at high office; the less the higher. It is the only refined way of avoiding scandals; nay, 'tis the shortest way back to good repute.

9. CULTIVATE THOSE WHO CAN TEACH YOU.

Let friendly intercourse be a school of knowledge, and culture be taught through conversation: thus you make your friends your teachers and mingle the pleasures of conversation with the advantages of instruction. Sensible persons thus enjoy alternating pleasures: they reap applause for what they say and gain instruction from what they hear. We are always attracted to others by our own interest, but in this case it is of a higher kind. Wise men frequent the houses of great noblemen not because they are temples of vanity, but as theatres of good breeding. There be gentlemen who have the credit of worldly wisdom because they are not only themselves oracles of all nobleness by their example and their behaviour, but those who surround them form a well-bred academy of worldly wisdom of the best and noblest kind.

14. THE THING ITSELF AND THE WAY IT IS DONE.

'Substance' is not enough: 'accident' is also required, as the scholastics say. A bad manner spoils everything, even reason and justice; a good one supplies everything, gilds a 'No', sweetens truth, and adds a touch of beauty to old age itself. The how plays a large part in affairs; a good manner steals into the affections. Fine behaviour is a joy in life, and a pleasant expression helps out of a difficulty in a remarkable way.

19. AROUSE NO EXAGGERATED EXPECTATIONS ON ENTERING.

It is the usual ill luck of all celebrities not to fulfil afterwards the expectations beforehand formed of them. The real can never equal the imagined, for it is easy to form ideals but very difficult to realise them. Imagination weds Hope and gives birth to much more than things are in themselves. However great the excellences, they never suffice to fulfil expectations, and as men find themselves disappointed with their exorbitant expectations they are more ready to be disillusioned than to admire. Hope is a great falsifier of truth; let skill guard against this by ensuring that fruition exceeds desire. A few creditable attempts at the beginning are sufficient to arouse curiosity without pledging one to the final object. It is better that reality should surpass the design and is better than was thought. This rule does not apply to the wicked, for the same exaggeration is a great aid to them; they are defeated amid general applause, and what seemed at first extreme ruin comes to be thought quite bearable.

23. BE SPOTLESS:

the indispensable condition of perfection. Few live without some weak point, either physical or moral, which they pamper because they could easily cure it. The keenness of others often regrets to see a slight defect attaching itself to a whole assembly of elevated qualities, and yet a single cloud can hide the whole of the sun. There are likewise patches on our reputation which ill will soon finds out and is continually noticing. The highest skill is to transform them into ornament. So Caesar hid his natural defects with the laurel.

26. FIND OUT EACH MAN'S THUMBSCREW.

'Tis the art of setting their wills in action. It needs more skill than resolution. You must know where to get at anyone. Every volition has a special motive which varies according to taste. All men are idolaters, some of fame, others of self-interest, most of pleasure. Skill consists in knowing these idols in order to bring them into play. Knowing any man's mainspring of motive you have as it were the key to his will. Have resort to primary motors, which are not always the highest but more often the lowest part of his nature: there are more dispositions badly organised than well. First guess a man's ruling passion, appeal to it by a word, set it in motion by temptation, and you will infallibly give checkmate to his freedom of will.

27. PRIZE INTENSITY MORE THAN EXTENT.

Excellence resides in quality, not in quantity. The best is always few and rare: much lowers value. Even among men giants are commonly the real dwarfs. Some reckon books by the thickness, as if they were written to try the brawn more than the brain. Extent alone never rises above mediocrity: it is the misfortune of universal geniuses that in attempting to be at home everywhere, are so nowhere. Intensity gives eminence and rises to the heroic in matters sublime.

31. SELECT THE LUCKY AND AVOID THE UNLUCKY.

Ill luck is generally the penalty of folly, and there is no disease so contagious to those who share in it. Never open the door to a lesser evil, for other and greater ones invariably slink in after it. The greatest skill at cards is to know when to discard; the smallest of current trumps is worth more than the ace of trumps of the last game. When in doubt, follow the suit of the wise and prudent; sooner or later they will win the odd trick.

32. HAVE THE REPUTATION OF BEING GRACIOUS.

'Tis the chief glory of the high and mighty to be gracious, a prerogative of kings to conquer universal goodwill. That is the great advantage of a commanding position – to be able to do more good than others. Those make friends who do friendly acts. On the other hand, there are some who lay themselves out for not being gracious, not on account of the difficulty, but from a bad disposition. In all things, they are the opposite of Divine grace.

38. LEAVE YOUR LUCK WHILE WINNING.

All the best players do it. A fine retreat is as good as a gallant attack. Bring your exploits under cover when there are enough, or even when there are many of them. Luck long lasting was ever suspicious; interrupted seems safer, and is even sweeter to the taste for a little infusion of bitter-sweet. The higher the heap of luck, the greater the risk of a slip, and down comes all. Fortune pays you sometimes for the intensity of her favours by the shortness of their duration. She soon tires of carrying any one long on her shoulders.

39. RECOGNISE WHEN THINGS ARE RIPE, AND THEN ENJOY THEM.

The works of nature all reach a certain point of maturity; up to that they improve, after that they degenerate. Few works of art reach such a point that they cannot be improved. It is an especial privilege of good taste to enjoy everything at its ripest. Not all can do this, nor do all who can know this. There is a ripening point too for fruits of intellect; it is well to know this both for their value in use and for their value in exchange.

43. THINK WITH THE FEW AND SPEAK WITH THE MANY.

By swimming against the stream it is impossible to remove error, easy to fall into danger; only a Socrates can undertake it. To dissent from others' views is regarded as an insult, because it is their condemnation. Disgust is doubled on account of the thing blamed and of the person who praised it. Truth is for the few, error is both common and vulgar. The wise man is not known by what he says on the housetops, for there he speaks not with his own voice but with that of common folly, however much his inmost thoughts may gainsay it. The prudent avoid being contradicted as much as contradicting: though they have their censure ready they are not ready to publish it. Thought is free, force cannot and should not be used to it. The wise man, therefore, retires into silence, and if he allows himself to come out of it, he does so in the shade and before few and fit persons.

52. NEVER BE PUT OUT.

'Tis a great aim of prudence never to be embarrassed. It is the sign of a real man, of a noble heart, for magnanimity is not easily put out. The passions are the humours of the soul, and every excess in them weakens prudence; if they overflow through the mouth, the reputation will be in danger. Let a man, therefore, be so much and so great a master over himself that neither in the most fortunate nor in the most adverse circumstances can anything cause his reputation injury by disturbing his self-possession, but rather enhance it by showing his superiority.

54. KNOW HOW TO SHOW YOUR TEETH.

Even hares can pull the mane of a dead lion. There is no joke about courage. Give way to the first and you must yield to the second, and so on till the last, and to gain your point at last costs as much trouble as would have gained much more at first. Moral courage exceeds physical; it should be like a sword kept ready for use in the scabbard of caution. It is the shield of great place; moral cowardice lowers one more than physical. Many have had eminent qualities, yet, for want of a stout heart, they passed inanimate lives and found a tomb in their own sloth. Wise Nature has thoughtfully combined in the bee the sweetness of its honey with the sharpness of its sting.

55. WAIT.

It's a sign of a noble heart dowered with patience, never to be in a hurry, never to be in a passion. First be master over yourself if you would be master over others. You must pass through the circumference of time before arriving at the centre of opportunity. A wise reserve seasons the aims and matures the means. Time's crutch effects more than the iron club of Hercules. God Himself chasteneth not with a rod but with time. He[1] spake a great word who said, 'Time and I against any two.' Fortune herself rewards waiting with the first prize.

1. Charles V.

56. HAVE PRESENCE OF MIND.

The child of a happy promptitude of spirit. Owing to this vivacity and wide-awakeness there is no fear of danger or mischance. Many reflect much only to go wrong in the end; others attain their aim without thinking of it beforehand. There are natures of antiperistasis[2] who work best in an emergency. They are like monsters who succeed in all they do offhand, but fail in aught they think over. A thing occurs to them at once or never: for them, there is no court of appeal. Celerity wins applause because it proves remarkable capacity; subtlety of judgment, prudence in action.

57. SLOW AND SURE.

Early enough if well. Quickly done can be quickly undone. To last an eternity requires an eternity of preparation. Only excellence counts; only achievement endures. Profound intelligence is the only foundation for immortality. Worth much costs much. The precious metals are the heaviest.

---

2. *Archaic:* resistance or reaction roused by opposition or by the action of an opposite principle or quality.

58. ADAPT YOURSELF TO YOUR COMPANY.

There is no need to show your ability before everyone. Employ no more force than is necessary. Let there be no unnecessary expenditure either of knowledge or of power. The skilful falconer only flies enough birds to serve for the chase. If there is too much display today there will be nothing to show tomorrow. Always have some novelty wherewith to dazzle. To show something fresh each day keeps expectation alive and conceals the limits of capacity.

59. FINISH OFF WELL.

In the House of Fortune, if you enter by the gate of pleasure you must leave by that of sorrow and vice versa. You ought, therefore, to think of the finish, and attach more importance to a graceful exit than to applause on entrance. 'Tis the common lot of the unlucky to have a very fortunate outset and a very tragic end. The important point is not the vulgar applause on entrance – that comes to nearly all – but the general feeling at exit. Few in life are felt to deserve an encore. Fortune rarely accompanies anyone to the door: warmly as she may welcome the coming, she speeds but coldly the parting guest.

63. TO BE THE FIRST OF THE KIND IS AN EXCELLENCE,

and to be eminent in it as well, a double one. To have the first move is a great advantage when the players are equal. Many a man would have been a veritable Phoenix if he had been the first of the sort. Those who come first are the heirs of Fame; the others get only a younger brother's allowance: whatever they do, they cannot persuade the world they are anything more than parrots. The skill of prodigies may find a new path to eminence, but prudence accompanies them all the way. By the novelty of their enterprises, sages write their names in the golden book of heroes. Some prefer to be first in things of minor import than second in greater exploits.

72. BE RESOLUTE.

Bad execution of your designs does less harm than irresolution in forming them. Streams do less harm flowing than when dammed up. There are some men so infirm of purpose that they always require direction from others, and this not on account of any perplexity, for they judge clearly, but from sheer incapacity for action. It needs some skill to find out difficulties, but more to find a way out of them. There are others who are never in straits: their clear judgment and determined character fit them for the highest callings; their intelligence tells them where to insert the thin end of the wedge, their resolution how to drive it home. They soon get through anything: as soon as they have done with one sphere of action, they are ready for another. Affianced to Fortune, they make themselves sure of success.

73. UTILISE SLIPS.

That is how smart people get out of difficulties. They extricate themselves from the most intricate labyrinth by some witty application of a bright remark. They get out of a serious contention by an airy nothing or by raising a smile. Most of the great leaders are well grounded in this art. When you have to refuse, it is often the polite way to talk of something else. Sometimes it proves the highest understanding not to understand.

74. DO NOT BE UNSOCIABLE.

The truest wild beasts live in the most populous places. To be inaccessible is the fault of those who distrust themselves, whose honours change their manners. It is no way of earning people's goodwill by being ill-tempered with them. It is a sight to see one of those unsociable monsters who make a point of being proudly impertinent. Their dependents, who have the misfortune to be obliged to speak with them, enter as if prepared for a fight with a tiger armed with patience and with fear. To obtain their post these persons must have ingratiated themselves with everyone, but having once obtained it they seek to indemnify themselves by disobliging all. It is a condition of their position that they should be accessible to all, yet, from pride or spleen, they are so to none. 'Tis a civil way to punish such men by letting them alone, and depriving them of opportunities of improvement by granting them no opportunity of intercourse.

77. BE ALL THINGS TO ALL MEN

– a discreet Proteus, learned with the learned, saintly with the sainted. It is the great art to gain everyone's suffrages; their goodwill gains general agreement. Notice men's moods and adapt yourself to each, genial or serious as the case may be. Follow their lead, glossing over the changes as cunningly as possible. This is an indispensable art for dependent persons. But this *savoir-faire* calls for great cleverness. He only will find no difficulty who has a universal genius in his knowledge and universal ingenuity in his wit.

81. RENEW YOUR BRILLIANCE.

'Tis the privilege of the Phoenix. Ability is wont to grow old, and with it fame. The staleness of custom weakens admiration, and a mediocrity that's new often eclipses the highest excellence grown old. Try therefore to be born again in valour, in genius, in fortune, in all. Display startling novelties, rise afresh like the sun every day. Change, too, the scene on which you shine, so that your loss may be felt in the old scenes of your triumph, while the novelty of your powers wins you applause in the new.

91. NEVER SET TO WORK AT ANYTHING IF YOU HAVE ANY DOUBTS OF ITS PRUDENCE.

A suspicion of failure in the mind of the doer is proof positive of it in that of the onlooker, especially if he is a rival. If in the heat of action your judgment feels scruples, it will afterwards in cool reflection condemn it as a piece of folly. Action is dangerous where prudence is in doubt: better leave such things alone. Wisdom does not trust to probabilities; it always marches in the mid-day light of reason. How can an enterprise succeed which the judgment condemns as soon as conceived? And if resolutions passed *nemine contradicente*[3] by inner court often turn out unfortunately, what can we expect of those undertaken by a doubting reason and a vacillating judgment?

3. Without a dissenting vote.

94. KEEP THE EXTENT OF YOUR ABILITIES UNKNOWN.

The wise man does not allow his knowledge and abilities to be sounded to the bottom, if he desires to be honoured by all. He allows you to know them but not to comprehend them. No one must know the extent of his abilities, lest he be disappointed. No one ever has an opportunity of fathoming him entirely. For guesses and doubts about the extent of his talents arouse more veneration than accurate knowledge of them, be they ever so great.

95. KEEP EXPECTATION ALIVE.

Keep stirring it up. Let much promise more, and great deeds herald greater. Do not rest your whole fortune on a single cast of the die. It requires great skill to moderate your forces so as to keep expectation from being dissipated.

106. DO NOT PARADE YOUR POSITION.

To outshine in dignity is more offensive than in personal attractions. To pose as a personage is to be hated: envy is surely enough. The more you seek esteem the less you obtain it, for it depends on the opinion of others. You cannot take it, but must earn and receive it from others. Great positions require an amount of authority sufficient to make them efficient:

without it, they cannot be adequately filled. Preserve therefore enough dignity to carry on the duties of the office. Do not enforce respect, but try and create it. Those who insist on the dignity of their office, show they have not deserved it, and that it is too much for them. If you wish to be valued, be valued for your talents, not for anything adventitious. Even kings prefer to be honoured for their personal qualifications rather than for their station.

114. NEVER COMPETE.

Every competition damages the credit: our rivals seize occasion to obscure us so as to outshine us. Few wage honourable war. Rivalry discloses faults which courtesy would hide. Many have lived in good repute while they had no rivals. The heat of conflict gives life, or even new life, to dead scandals, and digs up long-buried skeletons. Competition begins with belittling, and seeks aid wherever it can, not only where it ought. And when the weapons of abuse do not effect their purpose, as often or mostly happens, our opponents use them for revenge, and use them at least for beating away the dust of oblivion from anything to our discredit. Men of good will are always at peace; men of good repute and dignity are men of good will.

116. ONLY ACT WITH HONOURABLE MEN.

You can trust them and they you. Their honour is the best surety of their behaviour even in misunderstandings, for they always act having regard to what they are. Hence 'tis better to have a dispute with honourable people than to have a victory over dishonourable ones. You cannot treat with the ruined, for they have no hostages for rectitude. With them, there is no true friendship, and their agreements are not binding, however stringent they may appear, because they have no feeling of honour. Never have to do with such men, for if honour does not restrain a man, virtue will not, since honour is the throne of rectitude.

117. NEVER TALK OF YOURSELF.

You must either praise yourself, which is vain, or blame yourself, which is little-minded: it ill beseems him that speaks, and ill pleases him that hears. And if you should avoid this in ordinary conversation, how much more in official matters, and above all, in public speaking, where every appearance of unwisdom really is unwise. The same want of tact lies in speaking of a man in his presence, owing to the danger of going to one of two extremes: flattery or censure.

120. LIVE PRACTICALLY.

Even knowledge has to be in the fashion, and where it is not it is wise to affect ignorance. Thought and taste change with the times. Do not be old-fashioned in your ways of thinking, and let your taste be in the modern style. In everything the taste of the many carries the votes; for the time being one must follow it in the hope of leading it to higher things. In the adornment of the body as of the mind adapt yourself to the present, even though the past appear better. But this rule does not apply to kindness, for goodness is for all time. It is neglected nowadays and seems out of date. Truth-speaking, keeping your word, and so too good people, seem to come from the good old times: yet they are liked for all that, but in such a way that even when they all exist they are not in the fashion and are not imitated. What a misfortune for our age that it regards virtue as a stranger and vice as a matter of course! If you are wise, live as you can, if you cannot live as you would. Think more highly of what fate has given you than of what it has denied.

122. DISTINCTION IN SPEECH AND ACTION.

By this, you gain a position in many places and carry esteem beforehand. It shows itself in everything, in talk, in look, even in gait. It is a great victory to conquer men's hearts: it does not arise from any foolish presumption or pompous talk, but in a becoming tone of authority born of superior talent combined with true merit.

123. AVOID AFFECTATION.

The more merit, the less affectation, which gives a vulgar flavour to all. It is wearisome to others and troublesome to the one affected, for he becomes a martyr to care and tortures himself with attention. The most eminent merits lose most by it, for they appear proud and artificial instead of being the product of nature, and the natural is always more pleasing than the artificial. One always feels sure that the man who affects a virtue has it not. The more pains you take with a thing, the more should you conceal them, so that it may appear to arise spontaneously from your own natural character. Do not, however, in avoiding affectation fall into it by affecting to be unaffected. The sage never seems to know his own merits, for only by not noticing them can you call others' attention to them. He is twice great who has all the perfections in the opinion of all except himself; he attains applause by two opposite paths.

126. FOLLY CONSISTS NOT IN COMMITTING FOLLY, BUT IN NOT HIDING IT WHEN COMMITTED.

You should keep your desires sealed up, still more

your defects. All go wrong sometimes, but the wise try to hide the errors, but fools boast of them. Reputation depends more on what is hidden than on what is done; if a man does not live chastely, he must live cautiously. The errors of great men are like the eclipses of the greater lights. Even in friendship it is rare to expose one's failings to one's friend. Nay, one should conceal them from oneself if one can. But here one can help with that other great rule of life: learn to forget.

129. NEVER COMPLAIN.

To complain always brings discredit. Better be a model of self-reliance opposed to the passion of others than an object of their compassion. For it opens the way for the hearer to what we are complaining of, and to disclose one insult forms an excuse for another. By complaining of past offences we give occasion for future ones, and in seeking aid or counsel we only obtain indifference or contempt. It is much more politic to praise one man's favours, so that others may feel obliged to follow suit. To recount the favours we owe the absent is to demand similar ones from the present, and thus we sell our credit with the one to the other. The shrewd will therefore never publish to the world his failures or his defects, but only those marks of consideration which serve to keep friendship alive and enmity silent.

130. DO AND BE SEEN DOING.

Things do not pass for what they are but for what they seem. To be of use and to know how to show yourself of use, is to be twice as useful. What is not seen is as if it was not. Even the Right does not receive proper consideration if it does not seem right. The observant are far fewer in number than those who are deceived by appearances. Deceit rules the roost, things are judged by their jackets, and many things are other than they seem. A good exterior is the best recommendation of the inner perfection.

138. THE ART OF LETTING THINGS ALONE.

The more so the wilder the waves of public or of private life. There are hurricanes in human affairs, tempests of passion, when it is wise to retire to a harbour and ride at anchor. Remedies often make diseases worse: in such cases, one has to leave them to their natural course and the moral suasion of time. It takes a wise doctor to know when not to prescribe, and at times the greater skill consists in not applying remedies. The proper way to still the storms of the vulgar is to hold your hand and let them calm down of themselves. To give way now is to conquer by and by. A fountain gets muddy with but little stirring up, and does not get clear by our meddling with it but by our leaving it alone. The best remedy for disturbances is to let them run their course, for so they quiet down.

149. KNOW HOW TO PUT OFF ILLS ON OTHERS.

To have a shield against ill will is a great piece of skill in a ruler. It is not the resort of incapacity, as ill-wishers imagine, but is due to the higher policy of having someone to receive the censure of the disaffected and the punishment of universal detestation. Everything cannot turn out well, nor can everyone be satisfied: it is well, therefore, even at the cost of our pride, to have such a scapegoat, such a target for unlucky undertakings.

152. NEVER HAVE A COMPANION WHO CASTS YOU IN THE SHADE.

The more he does so, the less desirable a companion he is. The more he excels in quality the more in repute: he will always play first fiddle and you second. If you get any consideration, it is only his leavings. The moon shines bright alone among the stars: when the sun rises she becomes either invisible or imperceptible. Never join one that eclipses you, but rather one who sets you in a brighter light. By this means the cunning Fabula in Martial was able to appear beautiful and brilliant, owing to the ugliness and disorder of her companions. But one should as little imperil oneself by an evil companion as pay honour to another at the cost of one's own credit. When you are on the way to fortune, associate with the eminent; when arrived, with the mediocre.

153. BEWARE OF ENTERING WHERE THERE IS A GREAT GAP TO BE FILLED.

But if you do it be sure to surpass your predecessor; merely to equal him requires twice his worth. As it is a fine stroke to arrange that our successor shall cause us to be wished back, so it is policy to see that our predecessor does not eclipse us. To fill a great gap is difficult, for the past always seems best, and to equal the predecessor is not enough, since he has the right of first possession. You must, therefore, possess additional claims to oust the other from his hold on public opinion.

159. PUT UP WITH FOOLS.

The wise are always impatient, for he that increases knowledge increase impatience of folly. Much knowledge is difficult to satisfy. The first great rule of life, according to Epictetus, is to put up with things: he makes that the moiety of wisdom. To put up with all the varieties of folly would need much patience. We often have to put up with most from those on whom we most depend: a useful lesson in self-control. Out of patience comes forth peace, the priceless boon which is the happiness of the world. But let him that has no power of patience retire within himself, though even there he will have to put up with himself.

160. BE CAREFUL IN SPEAKING.

With your rivals from prudence; with others for the sake of appearance. There is always time to add a word, never to withdraw one. Talk as if you were making your will: the fewer words the less litigation. In trivial matters exercise yourself for the more weighty matters of speech. Profound secrecy has some of the lustre of the divine. He who speaks lightly soon falls or fails.

162. HOW TO TRIUMPH OVER RIVALS AND DETRACTORS.

It is not enough to despise them, though this is often wise: a gallant bearing is the thing. One cannot praise a man too much who speaks well of them who speak ill of him. There is no more heroic vengeance than that of talents and services which at once conquer and torment the envious. Every success is a further twist of the cord round the neck of the ill affected, and an enemy's glory is the rival's hell. The envious die not once, but as oft as the envied wins applause. The immortality of his fame is the measure of the other's torture: the one lives in endless honour, the other in endless pain. The clarion of Fame announces immortality to the one and death to the other, the slow death of envy long drawn out.

163. NEVER, FROM SYMPATHY WITH THE UNFORTUNATE, INVOLVE YOURSELF IN HIS FATE.

One man's misfortune is another man's luck, for one cannot be lucky without many being unlucky. It is a peculiarity of the unfortunate to arouse people's goodwill who desire to compensate them for the blows of fortune with their useless favour, and it happens that one who was abhorred by all in prosperity is adored by all in adversity. Vengeance on the wing is exchanged for compassion afoot. Yet 'tis to be noticed how fate shuffles the cards. There are men who always consort with the unlucky, and he that yesterday flew high and happy stands today miserable at their side. That argues nobility of soul, but not worldly wisdom.

169. BE MORE CAREFUL NOT TO MISS ONCE THAN TO HIT A HUNDRED TIMES.

No one looks at the blazing sun; all gaze when he is eclipsed. The common talk does not reckon what goes right but what goes wrong. Evil report carries farther than any applause. Many men are not known to the world till they have left it. All the exploits of a man taken together are not enough to wipe out a single small blemish. Avoid therefore falling into error, seeing that ill will notices every error and no success.

172. NEVER CONTEND WITH A MAN WHO HAS NOTHING TO LOSE;

for thereby you enter into an unequal conflict. The other enters without anxiety; having lost everything, including shame, he has no further loss to fear. He, therefore, resorts to all kinds of insolence. One should never expose a valuable reputation to so terrible a risk, lest what has cost years to gain may be lost in a moment, since a single slight may wipe out much sweat. A man of honour and responsibility has a reputation because he has much to lose. He balances his own and the other's reputation: he only enters into the contest with the greatest caution, and then goes to work with such circumspection that he gives time to prudence to retire in time and bring his reputation under cover. For even by victory he cannot gain what he has lost by exposing himself to the chances of loss.

177. AVOID FAMILIARITIES IN INTERCOURSE.

Neither use them nor permit them. He that is familiar loses any superiority his influence gives him, and so loses respect. The stars keep their brilliance by not making themselves common. The Divine demands decorum. Every familiarity breeds contempt. In human affairs, the more a man shows, the less he has, for in open communication you communicate the failings that reserve might keep under cover. Familiarity is never desirable; with superiors because it is dangerous, with inferiors because it is unbecoming, least of all with the common herd, who become insolent from sheer folly: they mistake favour shown them for need felt of them. Familiarity trenches on vulgarity.

181. THE TRUTH, BUT NOT THE WHOLE TRUTH.

Nothing demands more caution than the truth: 'tis the lancet of the heart. It requires as much to tell the truth as to conceal it. A single lie destroys a whole reputation for integrity. The deceit is regarded as treason and the deceiver as a traitor, which is worse. Yet not all truths can be spoken: some for our own sake, others for the sake of others.

183. DO NOT HOLD YOUR VIEWS TOO FIRMLY.

Every fool is fully convinced, and everyone fully persuaded is a fool: the more erroneous his judgment the more firmly he holds it. Even in cases of obvious certainty, it is fine to yield: our reasons for holding the view cannot escape notice, our courtesy in yielding must be the more recognised. Our obstinacy loses more than our victory yields: that is not to champion truth but rather rudeness. There be some heads of iron most difficult to turn: add caprice to obstinacy and the sum is a wearisome fool. Steadfastness should be for the will, not for the mind. Yet there are exceptions where one would fail twice, owning oneself wrong both in judgment and in the execution of it.

187. DO PLEASANT THINGS YOURSELF, UNPLEASANT THINGS THROUGH OTHERS.

By the one course you gain goodwill, by the other you avoid hatred. A great man takes more pleasure in doing a favour than in receiving one: it is the privilege of his generous nature. One cannot easily cause pain to another without suffering pain either from sympathy or from remorse. In high place one can only work by means of rewards and punishment, so grant the first yourself, inflict the other through others. Have someone against whom the weapons of discontent, hatred, and slander may be directed. For the rage of the mob is like that of a dog: missing the cause of its pain it turns to bite the whip itself, and though this is not the real culprit, it has to pay the penalty.

189. UTILISE ANOTHER'S WANTS.

The greater his wants the greater the turn of the screw. Philosophers say privation is non-existent, statesmen say it is all-embracing, and they are right. Many make ladders to attain their ends out of wants of others. They make use of the opportunity and tantalise the appetite by pointing out the difficulty of satisfaction. The energy of desire promises more than the inertia of possession. The passion of desire increases with every increase in opposition. It is a subtle point to satisfy the desire and yet preserve the dependence.

205. KNOW HOW TO PLAY THE CARD OF CONTEMPT.

It is a shrewd way of getting things you want, by affecting to depreciate them: generally they are not to be had when sought for, but fall into one's hands when one is not looking for them. As all mundane things are but shadows of the things eternal, they share with shadows this quality, that they flee from him who follows them and follow him that flees from them. Contempt is, besides, the most subtle form of revenge. It is a fixed rule with the wise never to defend themselves with the pen. For such defence always leaves a stain, and does more to glorify one's opponent than to punish his offence. It is a trick of the worthless to stand forth as opponents of great men, so as to win notoriety by a roundabout way, which they would never do by the straight road of merit. There are many we would not have heard of if their eminent opponents had not taken notice of them. There is no revenge like oblivion, through which they are buried in the dust of their unworthiness. Audacious persons hope to make themselves eternally famous by setting fire to one of the wonders of the world and of the ages. The art of reproving scandal is to take no notice of it, to combat it damages our own case; even if credited it causes discredit, and is a source of satisfaction to our opponent, for this shadow of a stain dulls the lustre of our fame even if it cannot altogether deaden it.

232. HAVE A TOUCH OF THE TRADER.

Life should not be all thought: there should be action as well. Very wise folk are generally easily deceived, for while they know out-of-the-way things they do not know the ordinary things of life, which are much more needful. The observation of higher things leaves them no time for things close at hand. Since they know not the very first thing they should know, and what everybody knows so well, they are either considered or thought ignorant by the superficial multitude. Let therefore the prudent take care to have something of the trader about him – enough to prevent him being deceived and so laughed at. Be a man adapted to the daily round, which if not the highest is the most necessary thing in life. Of what use is knowledge if it is not practical, and to know how to live is nowadays the true knowledge.

243. DO NOT BE TOO MUCH OF A DOVE.

Alternate the cunning of the serpent with the candour of the dove. Nothing is easier than to deceive an honest man. He believes in much who lies in naught; who does no deceit, has much confidence. To be deceived is not always due to stupidity, it may arise from sheer goodness. There are two sets of men who can guard themselves from injury: those who have experienced it at their own cost, and those who have observed it at the cost of others. Prudence should use as much suspicion as subtlety uses snares, and none need be so good as to enable others to do him ill. Combine in yourself the dove and the serpent, not as a monster but as a prodigy.

244. CREATE A FEELING OF OBLIGATION.

Some transform favours received into favours bestowed, and seem, or let it be thought, that they are doing a favour when receiving one. There are some so astute that they get honour by asking, and buy their own advantage with applause from others. They manage matters so cleverly that they seem to be doing others a service when receiving one from them. They transpose the order of obligation with extraordinary skill, or at least render it doubtful who has obliged whom. They buy the best by praising it, and make a flattering honour out of the pleasure they express. They oblige by their courtesy and thus make men beholden for what they themselves should be beholden. In this way they conjugate 'to oblige' in the active instead of in the passive voice, thereby proving themselves better politicians than grammarians. This is a subtle piece of *finesse*; a still greater is to perceive it, and to retaliate on such fools' bargains by paying in their own coin, and so coming buy your own again.

253. DO NOT EXPLAIN OVERMUCH.

Most men do not esteem what they understand, and venerate what they do not see. To be valued things should cost dear: what is not understood becomes overrated. You have to appear wiser and more prudent than he requires with whom you deal, if you desire to give him a high opinion of you; yet in this there should be moderation and no excess. And though with sensible people common sense holds its own, with most men a little elaboration is necessary. Give them no time for blame: occupy them with understanding your drift. Many praise a thing without being able to tell why, if asked. The reason is that they venerate the unknown as a mystery, and praise it because they hear it praised.

270. DO NOT CONDEMN ALONE THAT WHICH PLEASES ALL.

There must be something good in a thing that pleases so many; even if it cannot be explained it is certainly enjoyed. Singularity is always hated, and, when in the wrong, laughed at. You simply destroy respect for your taste rather than do harm to the object of your blame, and are left alone, you and your bad taste. If you cannot find the good in a thing, hide your incapacity and do not damn it straightway. As a general rule bad taste springs from want of knowledge. What all say, is so, or will be so.

276. KNOW HOW TO RENEW YOUR CHARACTER,

with the help both of Nature and of Art. Every seven years the disposition changes, they say. Let it be a change for the better and for the nobler in your taste. After the first seven comes reason, with each succeeding lustre let a new excellence be added. Observe this change so as to aid it, and hope also for betterment in others. Hence it arises that many change their behaviour when they change their position or their occupation. At times the change is not noticed till it reaches the height of maturity. At twenty Man is a Peacock, at thirty a Lion, at forty a Camel, at fifty a Serpent, at sixty a Dog, at seventy an Ape, at eighty nothing at all.

284. DO NOT BE IMPORTUNATE,

and so you will not be slighted. Respect yourself if you would have others respect you. Be sooner sparing than lavish with your presence. You will thus become desired and so well received. Never come unasked and only go when sent for. If you undertake a thing of your own accord you get all the blame if it fails, none of the thanks if it succeeds. The importunate is always the butt of blame, and because he thrusts himself in without shame he is thrust out with it.

285. NEVER DIE OF ANOTHER'S ILL-LUCK.

Notice those who stick in the mud, and observe how they call others to their aid so as to console themselves with a companion in misfortune. They seek someone to help them to bear misfortune, and often those who turned the cold shoulder on them in prosperity give them now a helping hand. There is great caution needed in helping the drowning without danger to oneself.

287. NEVER ACT IN A PASSION.

If you do, all is lost. You cannot act for yourself if you are not yourself, and passion always drives out reason. In such cases interpose a prudent go-between who can only be prudent if he keeps cool. That is why lookers-on see most of the game, because they keep cool. As soon as you notice that you are losing your temper beat a wise retreat. For no sooner is the blood up than it is spilt, and in a few moments occasion may be given for many days' repentance for oneself and complaints of the other party.

288. LIVE FOR THE MOMENT.

Our acts and thoughts and all must be determined by circumstances. Will when you may, for time and tide wait for no man. Do not live by certain fixed rules, except those that relate to the cardinal virtues. Nor let your will subscribe fixed conditions, for you may have to drink the water tomorrow which you cast away today. There be some so absurdly paradoxical that they expect all the circumstances of an action should bend to their eccentric whims and not vice versa. The wise man knows that the very polestar of prudence lies in steering by the wind.

297. ALWAYS ACT AS IF YOUR ACTS WERE SEEN.

He must see all around who sees that men see him or will see him. He knows that walls have ears and that ill deeds rebound back. Even when alone he acts as if the eyes of the whole world were upon him. For as he knows that sooner or later all will be known, so he considers those to be present as witnesses who must afterwards hear of the deed. He that wished the whole world might always see him did not mind that his neighbours could see him over their walls.

8

WILLIAM HAZLITT, ON SUCCESS

INTRODUCTION

'Success' literature typically displays a tendency that is at best idealistic, and at worst borderline dishonest.

It tells us to plan our time more effectively.

It tells us to develop our emotional intelligence.

It tells us to work harder, smarter, and more purposefully.

What the many rogues, chancers, and ne'er-do-wells who have progressed so handsomely in the world know is that this advice is, and has always been, a distraction from what really matters. Life has never been fair, predictable, or rational. The rules governing our advancement in the world follow quite another logic.

It is, however, rare for this logic to be spelt out – which is what makes William Hazlitt's 'On the Qualifications Necessary for Success' such an exceptional contribution to the underappreciated art of telling unsettling truths.

Hazlitt's first major insight is that people succeed in life as much through the qualifications they lack as through those they in fact possess. The way to secure success, he suggests, is to focus on obtaining it – rather than on deserving it. Pursuit of perfection only gets in the way; it is an obstacle to completing works, and beyond a certain point it only yields diminishing returns that cannot be appreciated by ordinary men. Breadth of talent doesn't help much either – to do anything well there should be 'an exclusiveness, a concentration, a bigotry, a blindness of attachment to that one object'. If you wish for success, strive to be the 'dull plodding man'; by being content with narrow mediocrity you are more likely to advance beyond it.

The second ingredient of success is what Hazlitt calls 'constitutional talent' – the vigour given to a man's ideas and pursuits by his bodily stamina and physical condition. It is better by far to have a weak mind in a sound body, says Hazlitt, than a sound mind and weak body. The man in robust physical condition 'shall strut and swagger and vapour and jostle his way through life, and have the upper-hand of those who are his betters in everything but health and strength'. The physically weak man, on the other hand, can never cast away his uneasy sense of personal insignificance and weakness. It avails little that there may be internal qualities since all that the observer sees is the exterior man. It is a man's strong body and vigorous constitution that is the best guarantor – and also the best criterion – of his progress through life.

The third ingredient is what Hazlitt calls 'animal spirits and showy accomplishment'. The world pays dividends to those who thrust themselves forward with aplomb: what wins out is not merely confidence but actual active impudence – the assumption of merit that is taken by observers to indicate its actual possession. Others take on trust the opinion we have of ourselves. The important thing is not to doubt your own pretensions, because providing you don't doubt yourself, no one else is likely to doubt you either. 'If you keep your own secret,' says Hazlitt, 'be assured the world will keep it for you.'

What's valuable about Hazlitt's perspective is its intense familiarity with the realities of life. The posture he adopts is not that of the lofty thinker peering down from his philosophical perch on a remote and inferior world. Instead, he throws us into the scrum of humanity: its arbitrariness, its hypocrisy, its cruelty, and its stupidity. And yet the tone of his essay is ultimately one of acknowledgement rather than of total rejection. The world of men is very far from perfect, the author seems to say. But it is our world. And it is a world that has its own comprehensible – if troubled – logic.

ON SUCCESS

It is curious to consider the diversity of men's talents, and the causes of their failure or success, which are not less numerous and contradictory than their pursuits in life. Fortune does not always smile on merit – 'the race is not to the swift, nor the battle to the strong'; and even where the candidate for wealth or honours succeeds, it is as often, perhaps, from the qualifications which he wants as from those which he possesses; or the eminence which he is lucky enough to attain is owing to some faculty or acquirement, which neither he nor any body else suspected. There is a balance of power in the human mind, by which defects frequently assist in furthering our views, as superfluous excellences are converted into the nature of impediments; and again, there is a continual substitution of one talent for another, through which we mistake the appearance for the reality, and judge (by implication) of the means from the end. So a Minister of State wields the House of Commons by his manner alone; while his friends and his foes are equally at a loss to account for his influence, looking for it in vain in the matter or style of his speeches. So the air with which a celebrated barrister waved a white cambric handkerchief passed for eloquence. So the buffoon is taken for a wit. To be thought wise, it is for the most part only necessary to seem so; and the noisy demagogue is easily translated, by the popular voice, into the orator and patriot. Qualities take their colour from those that are next them, as the chameleon borrows its hue from the nearest object; and unable otherwise to grasp the phantom of our choice or our ambition, we do well to lay violent hands on something else within our reach, which bears a general resemblance to it; and the impression of which, in proportion as the thing itself is cheap and worthless, is likely to be gross, obvious, striking, and effectual. The way to secure success is to be more anxious about obtaining than about deserving it; the surest hindrance to it is to have too high a standard of refinement in our own minds, or too high an opinion of the discernment of the public. He who is determined not to be satisfied with any thing short of perfection will never do any thing at all, either to please himself or others. The question is not what we ought to do, but what we can do for the best. An excess of modesty is, in fact, an excess of pride, and more hurtful to the individual, and less advantageous to society, than the grossest and most unblushing vanity –

Aspiring to be Gods, if angels fell,
Aspiring to be angels, men rebel.

If a celebrated artist in our own day had stayed to do justice to his principal figure in a generally admired painting before he had exhibited it, it would never have seen the light. He has passed on to other things more within his power to accomplish, and more within the competence of the spectators to understand. They see what he has done, which is a great deal – they could not have judged of, or given him credit for the ineffable idea in his own mind, which he might vainly have devoted his whole life in endeavouring to embody. The picture, as it is, is good enough for the age and for the public. If it had been ten times better, its merits would have been thrown away: if it had been ten times better in the more refined and lofty conception of character and sentiment, and had failed in the more palpable appeal to the senses and prejudices of the vulgar, in the usual 'appliances and means to boot', it would never have done. The work might have been praised by a few, a very few, and the artist himself have pined in penury and neglect. Mr Wordsworth has given us the essence of poetry in his works, without the machinery, the apparatus of poetical diction, the theatrical pomp, the conventional ornaments; and we see what he has made of it. The way to fame through merit alone is the narrowest, the steepest, the longest, the hardest of all others – that it is the most certain and lasting, is even a doubt – the most sterling reputation is, after all, but a species of imposture. As for ordinary cases of success and failure, they depend on the slightest shades of character or turn of accident – 'some trick not worth an egg' –

There's but the twinkling of a star
Betwixt a man of peace and war;
A thief and justice, fool and knave,
A huffing officer and a slave;
A crafty lawyer and pickpocket,
A great philosopher and a blockhead;
A formal preacher and a player,
A learn'd physician and manslayer.

Men are in numberless instances qualified for certain things for no other reason than because they are qualified for nothing else. Negative merit is the passport to negative success. In common life, the narrowness of our ideas and appetites is more favourable to the accomplishment of our designs, by confining our attention and ambition to one single object, than a greater enlargement of comprehension or susceptibility of taste, which (as far as the trammels of custom and routine of business are concerned) only operate as diversions to our ensuring the main chance; and, even in the pursuit of arts and science, a dull plodding fellow will often do better than one of a more mercurial and fiery cast – the mere unconsciousness of his own deficiencies, or of any thing beyond what he himself can do, reconciles him to his mechanical progress, and enables him to perform all that lies in his power with labour and patience. By being content with mediocrity, he advances beyond it; whereas the man of greater taste or genius may be supposed to fling down his pen or pencil in despair, haunted with the idea of unattainable excellence, and ends in being nothing, because he cannot be every thing at once. Those even who have done the greatest things were not always perhaps the greatest men. To do any given work, a man should not be greater in himself than the work he has to do; the faculties which he has beyond this will be faculties to let, either not used, or used idly and unprofitably, to hinder, not to help. To do any one thing best, there should be an exclusiveness, a concentration, a bigotry, a blindness of attachment to that one object; so that the widest range of knowledge and most diffusive subtlety of intellect will not uniformly produce the most beneficial results; and the performance is very frequently in the inverse ratio, not only of the pretensions, as we might superficially conclude, but of the real capacity. A part is greater than the whole: and this old saying seems to hold true in moral and intellectual questions also – in nearly all that relates to the mind of man, which cannot embrace the whole, but only a part.

I do not think (to give an instance or two of what I mean) that Milton's mind was (so to speak) greater than the *Paradise Lost*; it was just big enough to fill that mighty mould, the shrine contained the Godhead. Shakespeare's genius was, I should say, greater than any thing he has done, because it still soared free and unconfined beyond whatever he undertook – ran over, and could not be 'constrained by mastery' of his subject. Goldsmith, in his *Retaliation*, celebrates Burke as one who was kept back in his dazzling, wayward career, by the supererogation of his talents –

Though equal to all things, for all things unfit,
Too nice for a statesman, too proud for a wit.

Dr. Johnson, in Boswell's *Life*, tells us that the only person whose conversation he ever sought for improvement was George Psalmanazar: yet who knows any thing of this extraordinary man now, but that he wrote about twenty volumes of the Universal History – invented a Formosan alphabet and vocabulary – being a really learned man, contrived to pass for an impostor, and died no one knows how or where! The well-known author of the *Enquiry Concerning Political Justice*[1] in conversation has not a word to throw at a dog; all the stores of his understanding or genius he reserves for his books, and he has need of them, otherwise there would be hiatus in manuscripts. He says little, and that little were better left alone, being both dull and nonsensical; his talk is as flat as a pancake, there is no leaven in it, he has not dough enough to make a loaf and a cake; he has no idea of any thing till he is wound up, like a clock, not to speak, but to write, and then he seems like a person risen from sleep or

1. William Godwin.

from the dead. The author of the *Diversions of Purley*,[2] on the other hand, besides being the inventor of the theory of grammar, was a politician, a wit, a master of conversation, and overflowing with an interminable babble – that fellow had cut and come again in him, and

Tongue with a garnish of brains;

but it only served as an excuse to cheat posterity of the definition of a verb, by one of those conversational *ruses de guerre* by which he put off his guests at Wimbledon with some teasing equivoque[3] which he would explain the next time they met – and made him die at last with a nostrum in his mouth! The late Professor Porson was said to be a match for the Member for Old Sarum[4] in argument and raillery – he was a profound scholar, and had wit at will – yet what did it come to? His jests have evaporated with the marks of the wine on the tavern table; the page of Thucydides or Aeschylus, which was stamped on his brain, and which he could read there with equal facility backwards or forwards, is contained, after his death, as it was while he lived, just as well in the volume on the library shelf. The man[5] of perhaps the greatest ability now living is the one who has not only

2. John Horne Tooke.
3. An equivocal word or phrase; specifically: a pun.
4. William Pitt.
5. Samuel Taylor Coleridge.

done the least, but who is actually incapable of ever doing any thing worthy of him – unless he had a hundred hands to write with, and a hundred mouths to utter all that it hath entered into his heart to conceive, and centuries before him to embody the endless volume of his waking dreams. Cloud rolls over cloud; one train of thought suggests and is driven away by another; theory after theory is spun out of the bowels of his brain, not like the spider's web, compact and round, a citadel and a snare, built for mischief and for use; but, like the gossamer, stretched out and entangled without end, clinging to every casual object, flitting in the idle air, and glittering only in the ray of fancy. No subject can come amiss to him, and he is alike attracted and alike indifferent to all – he is not tied down to any one in particular – but floats from one to another, his mind every where finding its level, and feeling no limit but that of thought – now soaring with its head above the stars, now treading with fairy feet among flowers, now winnowing the air with winged words – passing from Duns Scotus to Jacob Behmen, from the Kantean philosophy to a conundrum, and from the Apocalypse to an acrostic – taking in the whole range of poetry, painting, wit, history, politics, metaphysics, criticism, and private scandal – every question giving birth to some new thought, and every thought 'discoursed in eloquent music', that lives only in the ear of fools, or in the report of absent friends. Set him to write a book, and he belies all that has been ever said about him –

Ten thousand great ideas filled his mind,
But with the clouds they fled, and left no trace behind.

Now there is ____, who never had an idea in his life, and who therefore has never been prevented by the fastidious refinements of self-knowledge, or the dangerous seductions of the Muse, from succeeding in a number of things which he has attempted, to the utmost extent of his dullness, and contrary to the advice and opinion of all his friends. He has written a book without being able to spell, by dint of asking questions – has painted draperies with great exactness, which have passed for finished portraits – daubs in an unaccountable figure or two, with a back-ground, and on due deliberation calls it history – he is dubbed an Associate after being twenty times black-balled, wins his way to the highest honours of the Academy, through all the gradations of discomfiture and disgrace, and may end in being made a foreign Count! And yet (such is the principle of distributive justice in matters of taste) he is just where he was. *Non ex quovis lingo fit Mercurius.*[6] Having once got an idea of ____, it is impossible that any thing he can do should ever alter it – though he were to paint like Raphael and Michelangelo, no one in the secret would give him credit for it, and 'though he had all knowledge,

6. A Mercury is not made out of any block of wood.

and could speak with the tongues of angels', yet without genius he would be nothing. The original sin of being what he is renders his good works and most meritorious efforts null and void. 'You cannot gather grapes of thorns, nor figs of thistles.' Nature still prevails over art. You look at _____, as you do at a curious machine, which performs certain puzzling operations, and as your surprise ceases, gradually unfolds other powers which you would little expect – but do what it will, it is but a machine still; the thing is without a soul!

Respice finem,[7] is the great rule in all practical pursuits: to attain our journey's end, we should look little to the right or to the left; the knowledge of excellence as often deters and distracts, as it stimulates the mind to exertion; and hence we may see some reason why the general diffusion of taste and liberal arts is not always accompanied with an increase of individual genius.

As there is a degree of dullness and phlegm, which, in the long run, sometimes succeeds better than the more noble and aspiring impulses of our nature (as the beagle by its sure tracing overtakes the bounding stag), so there is a degree of animal spirits and showy accomplishment which enables its possessors 'to get the start of the majestic world' and bear the palm alone. How often do we see vivacity and impertinence

---

7. 'Consider the end': live so that your life will be approved after your death; also: consider the consequences of your action.

mistaken for wit; fluency for argument; sound for sense; a loud or musical voice for eloquence! Impudence again is an equivalent for courage; and the assumption of merit and the possession of it are too often considered as one and the same thing. On the other hand, simplicity of manner reduces the person who cannot so far forego his native disposition as by any effort to shake it off, to perfect insignificance in the eyes of the vulgar, who, if you do not seem to doubt your own pretensions, will never question them; and on the same principle, if you do not try to palm yourself on them for what you are not, will never be persuaded you can be any thing. Admiration, like mocking, is catching; and the good opinion which gets abroad of us begins at home. If a man is not as much astonished at his own acquirements, as proud of and as delighted with the bauble, as others would be if put into sudden possession of it, they hold that true dessert and he must be strangers to each other; if he entertains an idea beyond his own immediate profession or pursuit, they think very wisely he can know nothing at all; if he does not play off the quack or the coxcomb upon them at every step, they are confident he is a dunce and a fellow of no pretensions. It has been sometimes made a matter of surprise that Mr Pitt did not talk politics out of the House; or that Mr Fox conversed like any one else on common subjects; or that Walter Scott is fonder of an old Scotch ditty or antiquarian record than of listening to the praises of the author of *Waverley*.[8] On the contrary, I cannot conceive how any one who feels conscious of certain powers should always be labouring to convince others of the fact; or how a person to whom their exercise is as familiar as the breath he draws should think it worth his while to convince them of what to him must seem so very simple, and at the same time so very evident. I should not wonder, however, if the author of the Scotch novels laid an undue stress on the praises of the monastery. We nurse the rickety child and prop up our want of self-confidence by the opinion of friends. A man (unless he is a fool) is never vain but when he stands in need of the tribute of adulation to strengthen the hollowness of his pretensions; nor conceited but when he can find no one to flatter him, and is obliged secretly to pamper his good opinion of himself to make up for the want of sympathy in others. A damned author has the highest sense of his own merits, and an inexpressible contempt for the judgment of his contemporaries; in the same manner that an actor who is hissed or hooted from the stage, creeps into exquisite favour with himself, in proportion to the blindness and injustice of the public. A prose writer, who has been severely handled in the reviews, will try to persuade himself that there is nobody else who can write a word of English; and we have seen a poet of our time, whose works have been much, but not (as he thought) sufficiently

8. Sir Walter Scott.

admired, undertake formally to prove that no poet who deserved the name of one was ever popular in his lifetime, or scarcely after his death!

There is nothing that floats a man sooner into the tide of reputation, or oftener passes current for genius, than what might be called constitutional talent. A man without this, whatever may be his worth or real powers, will no more get on in the world than a leaden Mercury will fly into the air; as any pretender with it, and with no one quality beside to recommend him, will be sure either to blunder upon success, or will set failure at defiance. By constitutional talent I mean, in general, the warmth and vigour given to a man's ideas and pursuits by his bodily stamina, by mere physical organisation. A weak mind in a sound body is better, or at least more profitable, than a sound mind in a weak and crazy conformation. How many instances might I quote! Let a man have a quick circulation, a good digestion, the bulk, and thews, and sinews of a man, and the alacrity, the unthinking confidence inspired by these; and without an atom, a shadow of the *mens divinior*,[9] he shall strut and swagger and vapour and jostle his way through life, and have the upper hand of those who are his betters in every thing but health and strength. His jests shall be echoed with loud laughter because his own lungs begin to crow like chanticleer[10]

9. A superior mind.
10. A name given to a rooster, especially in fairy tales.

before he has uttered them; while a little hectic nervous humourist shall stammer out an admirable conceit that is damned in the doubtful delivery – *vox faucibus haesit*.[11] The first shall tell a story as long as his arm, without interruption, while the latter stops short in his attempts from mere weakness of chest; the one shall be empty and noisy and successful in argument, putting forth the most commonplace things 'with a confident brow and a throng of words, that come with more than impudent sauciness from him', while the latter shrinks from an observation 'too deep for his hearers', into the delicacy and unnoticed retirement of his own mind. The one shall never feel the want of intellectual resources, because he can back his opinions with his person; the other shall lose the advantages of mental superiority, seek to anticipate contempt by giving offence, court mortification in despair of popularity, and even in the midst of public and private admiration, extorted slowly by incontrovertible proofs of genius, shall never get rid of the awkward, uneasy sense of personal weakness and insignificance, contracted by early and long-continued habit. What imports the inward to the outward man, when it is the last that is the general and inevitable butt of ridicule or object of admiration? It has been said that a good face is a letter of recommendation. But the finest face will not carry a man far unless it is set upon an active body and a

11. Voice stuck in throat.

153

stout pair of shoulders. The countenance is the index of a man's talents and attainments; his figure is the criterion of his progress through life. We may have seen faces that spoke 'a soul as fair –

Bright as the children of yon azure sheen' –

yet that met with but an indifferent reception in the world – and that being supported by a couple of spindle-shanks and a weak stomach, in fulfilling what was expected of them,

Fell flat, and shamed their worshippers.

Hence the successes of such persons did not correspond with their deserts. There was a natural contradiction between the physiognomy of their minds and bodies! The phrase, 'a good-looking man', means different things in town and country; and artists have a separate standard of beauty from other people. A country squire is thought good looking, who is in good condition like his horse: a country farmer, to take the neighbours' eyes, must seem stall-fed, like the prize ox; they ask, 'how he cuts up in the caul, how he tallows in the kidneys'. The letter-of-recommendation face, in general, is not one that expresses the finer movements of thought or of the soul, but that makes part of a vigorous and healthy form. It is one in which Cupid and Mars take up their quarters, rather than Saturn or Mercury. It may be objected here that some of the greatest favourites of fortune have been little men. 'A little man, but of high fancy', is Sterne's description of Mr Hammond Shandy. But then they have been possessed of strong fibres and an iron constitution. The late Mr West said that Bonaparte was the best-made man he ever saw in his life. In other cases, the gauntlet of contempt which a puny body and a fiery spirit are forced to run may determine the possessors to aim at great actions; indignation may make men heroes as well as poets, and thus revenge them on the niggardliness of nature and the prejudices of the world. I remember Mr Wordsworth's saying that he thought ingenious poets had been of small and delicate frames, like Pope; but that the greatest (such as Shakespeare and Milton) had been healthy, and cast in a larger and handsomer mould. So were Titian, Raphael, and Michelangelo. This is one of the few observations of Mr Wordsworth's I recollect worth quoting, and I accordingly set it down as his, because I understand he is tenacious on that point.

In love, in war, in conversation, in business, confidence and resolution are the principal things. Hence the poet's reasoning:

For women, born to be controll'd,
Affect the loud, the vain, the bold.

Nor is this peculiar to them, but runs all through life. It is the opinion we appear to entertain of ourselves, from which (thinking we must be the best judges of our own merits) others accept their idea of us on trust. It is taken for granted that everyone pretends to the utmost he can do, and he who pretends to little is supposed capable of nothing. The humility of our approaches to power or beauty ensures a repulse, and the repulse makes us unwilling to renew the application; for there is pride as well as humility in this habitual backwardness and reserve. If you do not bully the world, they will be sure to insult over you, because they think they can do it with impunity. They insist upon the arrogant assumption of superiority somewhere, and if you do not prevent them, they will practise it on you. Some one must top the part of Captain in the play. Servility, however, chimes in, and plays Scrub[12] in the farce. Men patronise the fawning and obsequious, as they submit to the vain and boastful. It is the air of modesty and independence, which will neither be put upon itself, nor put upon others, that they cannot endure – that excites all the indignation they should feel for pompous affectation, and all the contempt they do not show to meanness and duplicity. Our indolence and perhaps our envy take part with our cowardice and vanity in all this. The obtrusive claims of empty ostentation, played off like the ring on the finger, fluttering and sparkling in our sight, relieve us from the irksome task of seeking out obscure merit; the scroll of virtues written on the

12. The servant.

bold front, or triumphing in the laughing eye, save us the trouble of sifting the evidence and deciding for ourselves; besides, our self-love receives a less sensible shock from encountering the mere semblance than the solid substance of worth; folly chuckles to find the blockhead put over the wise man's head, and cunning winks to see the knave, by his own good leave, transformed into a saint.

Doubtless, the pleasure is as great
In being cheated, as to cheat.

In all cases, there seems a sort of compromise, a principle of collusion between imposture and credulity. If you ask what sort of adventurers have swindled tradesmen of their goods, you will find they are all likely men, with plausible manners or a handsome equipage, hired on purpose – if you ask what sort of gallants have robbed women of their hearts, you will find they are those who have jilted hundreds before, from which the willing fair conceives the project of fixing the truant to herself – so the bird flutters its idle wings in the jaws of destruction, and the foolish moth rushes into the flame that consumes it! There is no trusting to appearances, we are told; but this maxim is of no avail, for men are the eager dupes of them. Life, it has been said, is 'the art of being well deceived'; and accordingly, hypocrisy seems to be the great business of mankind. The game of fortune is, for the most part, set up with counters; so that he who will not cut in because he has no gold in his pocket, must sit out above half his time, and lose his chance of sweeping the tables. Delicacy is, in ninety-nine cases out of a hundred, considered as rusticity; and sincerity of purpose is the greatest affront that can be offered to society. To insist on simple truth, is to disqualify yourself for place or patronage – the less you deserve, the more merit in their encouraging you; and he who, in the struggle for distinction, trusts to realities and not to appearances will, in the end, find himself the object of universal hatred and scorn. A man who thinks to gain and keep the public ear by the force of style will find it very uphill work; if you wish to pass for a great author, you ought not to look as if you were ignorant that you had ever written a sentence or discovered a single truth. If you keep your own secret, be assured the world will keep it for you. A writer, whom I know very well, cannot gain an admission to Drury Lane Theatre, because he does not lounge into the lobbies, or sup at the Shakespeare – nay, the same person having written upwards of sixty columns of original matter on politics, criticism, belles-lettres, and *virtù* in a respectable morning paper, in a single half-year, was, at the end of that period, on applying for a renewal of his engagement, told by the editor 'he might give in a specimen of what he could do!' One would think sixty columns of the *Morning Chronicle* were a sufficient specimen of what a man could do. But while this person was thinking of his next answer to Vetus,[13] or his account of Mr Kean's performance of *Hamlet*, he had neglected 'to point the toe', to hold up his head higher than usual (having acquired a habit of poring over books when young), and to get a new velvet collar to an old-fashioned great coat. These are 'the graceful ornaments to the columns of a newspaper – the Corinthian capitals of a polished style!' This unprofitable servant of the press found no difference in himself before or after he became known to the readers of the *Morning Chronicle*, and it accordingly made no difference in his appearance or pretensions. 'Don't you remember', says Gray, in one of his letters, 'Lord C and Lord M who are now great statesmen, little dirty boys playing at cricket? For my own part, I don't feel myself a bit taller, or older, or wiser, than I did then.' It is no wonder that a poet, who thought in this manner of himself, was hunted from college to college, has left us so few precious specimens of his fine powers, and shrunk from his reputation into a silent grave!

'I never knew a man of genius a coxcomb in dress', said a man of genius and a sloven in dress. I do know a man of genius who is a coxcomb in his dress, and in everything else. But let that pass.

C'est un mauvais métier que celui de médire.[14]

I also know an artist who has at least the ambition

---

13. The Irish journalist Edward Sterling.
14. *It's as nasty a job as speaking ill of someone.*

and the boldness of genius, who has been reproached with being a coxcomb, and with affecting singularity in his dress and demeanour. If he is a coxcomb that way, he is not so in himself, but a rattling hair-brained fellow, with a great deal of unconstrained gaiety, and impetuous (not to say turbulent) life of mind! Happy it is when a man's exuberance of self-love flies off to the circumference of a broad-brimmed hat, descends to the toes of his shoes, or carries itself off with the peculiarity of his gait, or even vents itself in a little professional quackery – and when he seems to think sometimes of you, sometimes of himself, and sometimes of others, and you do not feel it necessary to pay to him all the finical devotion, or to submit to be treated with the scornful neglect of a proud beauty, or some Prince Prettyman. It is well to be something besides the coxcomb, for our own sake as well as that of others; but to be born wholly without this faculty or gift of Providence, a man had better have had a stone tied about his neck, and been cast into the sea.

In general, the consciousness of internal power leads rather to a disregard of, than a studied attention to, external appearance. The wear and tear of the mind does not improve the sleekness of the skin, or the elasticity of the muscles. The burthen of thought weighs down the body like a porter's burthen. A man cannot stand so upright or move so briskly under it as if he had nothing to carry in his head or on his shoulders. The rose on the cheek and the canker at the heart do not flourish at the same time; and he who has much to think of, must take many things to heart; for thought and feeling are one. He who can truly say, *Nihil humani a me alienum puto*,[15] has a world of cares on his hands, which nobody knows anything of but himself. This is not one of the least miseries of a studious life. The common herd do not by any means give him full credit for his gratuitous sympathy with their concerns; but are struck with his lacklustre eye and wasted appearance. They cannot translate the expression of his countenance out of the vulgate; they mistake the knitting of his brows for the frown of displeasure, the paleness of study for the languor of sickness, the furrows of thought for the regular approaches of old age. They read his looks, not his books; have no clue to penetrate the last recesses of the mind, and attribute the height of abstraction to more than an ordinary share of stupidity. 'Mr. Hazlitt never seems to take the slightest interest in any thing,' is a remark I have often heard made in a whisper. People do not like your philosopher at all, for he does not look, say, or think as they do; and they respect him still less. The majority go by personal appearances, not by proofs of intellectual power; and they are quite right in this, for they are better judges of the one than of the other. There is a large party who undervalue Mr. Kean's[16]

---

15. I regard nothing human as foreign to me.
16. Edmund Kean.

acting (and very properly, as far as they are concerned) for they can see that he is a little ill-made man, but they are incapable of entering into the depth and height of the passion in his Othello. A nobleman of high rank, sense, and merit, who had accepted an order of knighthood, on being challenged for so doing by a friend, as a thing rather degrading to him than otherwise, made answer – 'What you say, may be very true; but I am a little man, and am sometimes jostled, and treated with very little ceremony in walking along the streets; now the advantage of this new honour will be that when people see the star at my breast, they will every one made way for me with the greatest respect.' Pope bent himself double and ruined his constitution by over-study when young. He was hardly indemnified by all his posthumous fame, 'the flattery that soothes the dull cold ear of death', nor by the admiration of his friends, nor the friendship of the great, for the distortion of his person, the want of robust health, and the insignificant figure he made in the eyes of strangers, and of Lady Mary Wortley Montague.[17] Not only was his diminutive and misshapen form against him in such trivial toys, but it was made a set-off and a bar to his poetical pretensions by his brother-poets, who ingeniously converted the initial and final letters of his name into the invidious appellation A.P.E. He probably had the passage made underground from his

---

17. When Pope declared his love for her she responded with laughter.

garden to his grotto, that he might not be rudely gazed at in crossing the road by some untutored clown; and perhaps started to see the worm he trod upon writhed into his own form, like Elshie the Black Dwarf.[18] Let those who think the mind everything and the body nothing, 'ere we have shuffled off this mortal coil', read that fine moral fiction, or the real story of David Ritchie – believe and tremble![19]

It may be urged that there is a remedy for all this in the appeal from the ignorant many to the enlightened few. But the few who are judges of what is called real and solid merit are not forward to communicate their occult discoveries to others; they are withheld partly by envy, and partly by pusillanimity. The strongest minds are by rights the most independent and ingenious; but then they are competitors in the lists, and jealous of the prize. The prudent (and the wise are prudent!) only add their hearty applause to the acclamations of the multitude, which they can neither

18. From Walter Scott's novel, *The Black Dwarf*.

19. Hazlitt: 'It is more desirable to be the handsomest than the wisest man in Majesty's dominions, for there are more people who have eyes than understandings. Sir John Suckling tell us that 'He prized black eyes and a lucky hit/At bowls, above all the trophies of wit.' In like manner, I would be permitted to say, that I am somewhat sick of this trade of authorship, where the critics look askance at one's best-meant efforts, but am still fond of those athletic exercises, where they do not keep two scores to mark the game, with Whig and Tory notches. The accomplishments of the body are obvious and clear to all: those of the mind are recondite and doubtful, and therefore grudgingly acknowledged, or held up as the sport of prejudice, spite, and folly.'

silence nor dispute. So Mr. Gifford dedicated those verses to Mr. Hoppner, when securely seated on the heights of fame and fortune, which before he thought might have savoured too much of flattery or friendship. Those even who have the sagacity to discover it seldom volunteer to introduce obscure merit into publicity, so as to endanger their own pretensions: they praise the world's idols, and bow down at the altars which they cannot overturn by violence or undermine by stealth! Suppose literary men to be the judges and vouchers for literary merit – but it may sometimes happen that a literary man (however high in genius or in fame) has no passion but the love of distinction, and hates every person or thing that interferes with his inadmissible and exorbitant claims. Dead to every other interest, he is alive to that, and starts up, like a serpent when trod upon, out of the slumber of wounded pride. The cold slime of indifference is turned into rank poison at the sight of your approach to an equality or competition with himself. If he is an old acquaintance, he would keep you always where you were, under his feet to be trampled on; if a new one, he wonders he never heard of you before. As you become known, he expresses a greater contempt for you, and grows more captious and uneasy. The more you strive to merit his good word, the farther you are from it. Such characters will not only sneer at your well-meant endeavours, and keep silent as to your good qualities, but are out of countenance, 'quite chop-fallen', if they find you have a cup of water, or a crust of bread. It is only when you are in a jail, starved or dead, that their exclusive pretensions are safe, or their Argus-eyed suspicions laid asleep. This is a true copy, nor is it taken from one sitting, or a single subject. An author nowadays to succeed must be something more than an author – a nobleman, or rich plebeian; the simple literary character is not enough. 'Such a poor forked animal', as a mere poet or philosopher turned loose upon public opinion, has no chance against the flocks of bats and owls that instantly assail him. It is name, it is wealth, it is title and influence that mollifies the tender-hearted Cerberus[20] of criticism – first, by placing the honorary candidate for fame out of the reach of Grub-street malice; secondly, by holding out the prospect of a dinner or a vacant office to successful sycophancy. This is the reason why a certain magazine praises Percy Bysshe Shelley, and vilifies 'Johnny Keats':[21] they know very well that they cannot ruin the one in fortune as well as in fame, but they may ruin the other in both, deprive him of a livelihood together with his good name, send him to Coventry,[22] and into the rules of a prison; and this is a double incitement to the exercise of their laudable and legitimate vocation. We do not hear that they plead the good-natured motive of the editor of the

---

20. A three-headed dog that in Greek mythology guards the entrance to Hades.
21. Hazlitt: 'Written in June 1820.'
22. 'To send to Coventry': to ostracize.

Quarterly Review, that 'they did it for his good', because someone, in consequence of that critic's abuse, had sent the author a present of five-and-twenty pounds! One of these writers went so far, in a sort of general profession of literary servility, as to declare broadly that there had been no great English poet, and that no one had a right to pretend to the character of a man of genius in this country who was not of patrician birth – or connections by marriage! This hook was well baited.

> *These are the doctrines that enrich the shops,*
> *That pass with reputation through the land,*
> *And bring their authors an immortal name.*

It is the sympathy of the public with the spite, jealousy, and irritable humours of the writers, that nourishes this disease in the public mind; this, this 'embalms and spices to the April day again', what otherwise 'the spital[23] and the lazar-house[24] would heave the gorge at!'

23. Hospital.
24. Leper colony.

FRIEDRICH NIETZSCHE, BEYOND GOOD AND EVIL

INTRODUCTION

Nietzsche was one of the first great radical traditionalists. He believed that recent human history had been little more than an evolution towards mediocrity. And he thought he could point to a way out.

One of Nietzsche's major projects was to construct what he called a 'genealogy of morals' – an account of the origin and history of moral values. Moral values are not, he said, objective and universal. Instead, they are relative and local. Broadly speaking, morality can be divided into two opposing types – master morality and slave morality.

Master morality is morality as determined by the ruling caste. When rulers determine what is meant by 'good', they refer to 'the exalted, proud disposition' that characterises their own caste. When they determine what is meant by 'bad', they refer to all that they hold in contempt and disregard: the cowardly, the timid, the insignificant, and the self-abasing. Under this moral view, the antithesis 'good' and 'bad' means, in practice, the same as 'noble' and 'despicable'.

Slave morality starts out from a fundamentally different point of origin – the perspective of the oppressed, the suffering, the unemancipated, and the weary. The moral viewpoint of this group will develop along a very different path. The oppressed will adopt a pessimistic suspicion towards man's condition and perhaps condemn it outright. In this context, it is the qualities that alleviate the existence of sufferers that will be constituted as the 'good': sympathy, the helping hand, the warm heart, patience, diligence, humility, and friendliness. These are the most useful qualities and the only means of supporting the burden of existence.

A more profound distinction can be found in the source of value judgments. The nobler type of man regards himself as the determiner of values. He does not require to be approved of; instead, he passes the judgment. And he honours what he recognises in himself. The slavish type of man, on the other hand, seeks to elicit good opinions of himself from others, rejoicing over every good opinion and suffering from every bad one. This is the oldest instinct of subjection and it survives in the blood as vanity.

To grasp the full reach of this philosophy, you have to understand that insofar as master morality and slave morality exist today, they do so not by way of literal 'masters' and 'slaves' but rather in tendencies and orientations of the human soul. Nietzsche was very specific about this: he thought that the two moralities have often been found confused and juxtaposed within the same man. What is in issue, then, is no longer the morality of the nobility as a caste, but rather the predominance of the nobler tendencies within the individual soul.

It is in this respect that Nietzsche is a source of real insight for the modern man. It is true that what he has to say about the decline of man and the rise of the cult of mediocrity provides a valuable check and counterpoise to the excesses of progressivism. It is also true that what he has to say about the relativity of morals gives proper perspective to value judgments that so often function as a cover story and vehicle for self-interest. But these are secondary benefits.

The primary benefit for the modern man is the self-grounding that Nietzsche's analysis can provide. There is no ascertainable objective basis for your values, he insists. Everyone is alone in a universe of exploitation and predation. Respond, then, as a man noble in soul would do. That means no more abjection and no more 'self-dwarfing'. It means looking forward to building your own future rather than upwards for approval. And, above all, it means becoming a determiner of your own values and serving the universe not out of pity, but from a feeling of abundance, strength, and healthy self-love.

CHAPTER 9

WHAT IS NOBLE?

257. Every elevation of the type 'man' has hitherto been the work of an aristocratic society and so it will always be – a society believing in a long scale of gradations of rank and differences of worth among human beings, and requiring slavery in some form or other. Without the *pathos of distance*, such as grows out of the incarnated difference of classes, out of the constant out-looking and down-looking of the ruling caste on subordinates and instruments, and out of their equally constant practice of obeying and commanding, of keeping down and keeping at a distance – that other more mysterious pathos could never have arisen, the longing for an ever new widening of distance within the soul itself, the formation of ever higher, rarer, further, more extended, more comprehensive states, in short, just

the elevation of the type 'man', the continued 'self-surmounting of man', to use a moral formula in a supermoral sense. To be sure, one must not resign oneself to any humanitarian illusions about the history of the origin of an aristocratic society (that is to say, of the preliminary condition for the elevation of the type 'man'): the truth is hard. Let us acknowledge unprejudicedly how every higher civilization hitherto has *originated*! Men with a still natural nature, barbarians in every terrible sense of the word, men of prey, still in possession of unbroken strength of will and desire for power, threw themselves upon weaker, more moral, more peaceful races (perhaps trading or cattle-rearing communities), or upon old mellow civilizations in which the final vital force was flickering out in brilliant fireworks of wit and depravity. At the commencement, the noble caste was always the barbarian caste: their superiority did not consist first of all in their physical, but in their psychical power – they were more *complete* men (which at every point also implies the same as 'more complete beasts').

258. Corruption – as the indication that anarchy threatens to break out among the instincts, and that the foundation of the emotions, called 'life', is convulsed – is something radically different according to the organization in which it manifests itself. When, for instance, an aristocracy like that of France at the beginning of the Revolution flung away its privileges with sublime disgust and sacrificed itself to an excess

of its moral sentiments, it was corruption: it was really only the closing act of the corruption which had existed for centuries, by virtue of which that aristocracy had abdicated step by step its lordly prerogatives and lowered itself to a *function* of royalty (in the end even to its decoration and parade-dress). The essential thing, however, in a good and healthy aristocracy is that it should *not* regard itself as a function either of the kingship or the commonwealth, but as the *significance* and highest justification thereof – that it should therefore accept with a good conscience the sacrifice of a legion of individuals, who, *for its sake*, must be suppressed and reduced to imperfect men, to slaves and instruments. Its fundamental belief must be precisely that society is *not* allowed to exist for its own sake, but only as a foundation and scaffolding, by means of which a select class of beings may be able to elevate themselves to their higher duties, and in general to a higher *existence*: like those sun-seeking climbing plants in Java – they are called *Sipo Matador* – which encircle an oak so long and so often with their arms, until at last, high above it, but supported by it, they can unfold their tops in the open light, and exhibit their happiness.

259. To refrain mutually from injury, from violence, from exploitation, and put one's will on a par with that of others: this may result in a certain rough sense in good conduct among individuals when the necessary conditions are given (namely, the actual

similarity of the individuals in amount of force and degree of worth, and their co-relation within one organization). As soon, however, as one wished to take this principle more generally, and if possible even as *the fundamental principle of society*, it would immediately disclose what it really is – namely, a Will to the *denial* of life, a principle of dissolution and decay. Here one must think profoundly to the very basis and resist all sentimental weakness: life itself is *essentially* appropriation, injury, conquest of the strange and weak, suppression, severity, obtrusion of peculiar forms, incorporation, and at the least, putting it mildest, exploitation – but why should one for ever use precisely these words on which for ages a disparaging purpose has been stamped? Even the organization within which, as was previously supposed, the individuals treat each other as equal – it takes place in every healthy aristocracy – must itself, if it be a living and not a dying organization, do all that towards other bodies which the individuals within it refrain from doing to each other: it will have to be the incarnated Will to Power, it will endeavour to grow, to gain ground, attract to itself and acquire ascendancy – not owing to any morality or immorality, but because it *lives*, and because life *is* precisely Will to Power. On no point, however, is the ordinary consciousness of Europeans more unwilling to be corrected than on this matter; people now rave everywhere, even under the guise of science, about coming conditions of society in which 'the exploiting character' is to be absent – that sounds to my ears as if they promised to invent a mode of life which should refrain from all organic functions. 'Exploitation' does not belong to a depraved, or imperfect and primitive society: it belongs to the *nature* of the living being as a primary organic function; it is a consequence of the intrinsic Will to Power, which is precisely the Will to Life. Granting that as a theory this is a novelty – as a reality it is the *fundamental fact* of all history: let us be so far honest towards ourselves!

260. In a tour through the many finer and coarser moralities which have hitherto prevailed or still prevail on the earth, I found certain traits recurring regularly together, and connected with one another, until finally two primary types revealed themselves to me, and a radical distinction was brought to light. There is *master-morality* and *slave-morality* – I would at once add, however, that in all higher and mixed civilizations, there are also attempts at the reconciliation of the two moralities, but one finds still oftener the confusion and mutual misunderstanding of them, indeed sometimes their close juxtaposition – even in the same man, within one soul. The distinctions of moral values have either originated in a ruling caste, pleasantly conscious of being different from the ruled – or among the ruled class, the slaves and dependents of all sorts. In the first case, when it is the rulers who determine the conception 'good', it is the exalted, proud disposition which is regarded as the distinguishing feature, and that which determines

the order of rank. The noble type of man separates from himself the beings in whom the opposite of this exalted, proud disposition displays itself: he despises them. Let it at once be noted that in this first kind of morality the antithesis 'good' and 'bad' means practically the same as 'noble' and 'despicable' – the antithesis 'good' and '*evil*' is of a different origin. The cowardly, the timid, the insignificant, and those thinking merely of narrow utility are despised; moreover, also, the distrustful, with their constrained glances, the self-abasing, the dog-like kind of men who let themselves be abused, the mendicant flatterers, and above all the liars – it is a fundamental belief of all aristocrats that the common people are untruthful. 'We truthful ones' – the nobility in ancient Greece called themselves. It is obvious that everywhere the designations of moral value were at first applied to *men*; and were only derivatively and at a later period applied to *actions*; it is a gross mistake, therefore, when historians of morals start with questions like, 'Why have sympathetic actions been praised?' The noble type of man regards *himself* as a determiner of values; he does not require to be approved of; he passes the judgment: 'What is injurious to me is injurious in itself'; he knows that it is he himself only who confers honour on things; he is a *creator of values*. He honours whatever he recognizes in himself: such morality equals self-glorification. In the foreground there is the feeling of plenitude, of power, which seeks to overflow, the happiness of high tension, the consciousness of a wealth which would fain give and bestow: the noble man also helps the unfortunate, but not – or scarcely – out of pity, but rather from an impulse generated by the super-abundance of power. The noble man honours in himself the powerful one, him also who has power over himself, who knows how to speak and how to keep silence, who takes pleasure in subjecting himself to severity and hardness, and has reverence for all that is severe and hard. 'Wotan placed a hard heart in my breast', says an old Scandinavian Saga: it is thus rightly expressed from the soul of a proud Viking. Such a type of man is even proud of not being made for sympathy; the hero of the Saga therefore adds warningly: 'He who has not a hard heart when young, will never have one'. The noble and brave who think thus are the furthest removed from the morality which sees precisely in sympathy, or in acting for the good of others, or in *desinteressement*,[1] the characteristic of the moral; faith in oneself, pride in oneself, a radical enmity and irony towards 'selflessness', belong as definitely to noble morality, as do a careless scorn and precaution in presence of sympathy and the 'warm heart'. It is the powerful who *know* how to honour, it is their art, their domain for invention. The profound reverence for age and for tradition – all law rests on this double reverence – the belief and prejudice in favour of ancestors and

1. Selflessness.

unfavourable to newcomers, is typical in the morality of the powerful; and if, reversely, men of 'modern ideas' believe almost instinctively in 'progress' and the 'future', and are more and more lacking in respect for old age, the ignoble origin of these 'ideas' has complacently betrayed itself thereby. A morality of the ruling class, however, is more especially foreign and irritating to present-day taste in the sternness of its principle that one has duties only to one's equals; that one may act towards beings of a lower rank, towards all that is foreign, just as seems good to one, or 'as the heart desires', and in any case 'beyond good and evil': it is here that sympathy and similar sentiments can have a place. The ability and obligation to exercise prolonged gratitude and prolonged revenge – both only within the circle of equals – artfulness in retaliation, *raffinement*[2] of the idea in friendship, a certain necessity to have enemies (as outlets for the emotions of envy, quarrelsomeness, arrogance – in fact, in order to be a good *friend*): all these are typical characteristics of the noble morality, which, as has been pointed out, is not the morality of 'modern ideas', and is therefore at present difficult to realize, and also to unearth and disclose. It is otherwise with the second type of morality, *slave-morality*. Supposing that the abused, the oppressed, the suffering, the unemancipated, the weary, and those uncertain of themselves should moralize, what

2. Refinement.

177

will be the common element in their moral estimates? Probably a pessimistic suspicion with regard to the entire situation of man will find expression, perhaps a condemnation of man, together with his situation. The slave has an unfavourable eye for the virtues of the powerful; he has a skepticism and distrust, a *refinement* of distrust of everything 'good' that is there honoured – he would fain persuade himself that the very happiness there is not genuine. On the other hand, *those* qualities which serve to alleviate the existence of sufferers are brought into prominence and flooded with light; it is here that sympathy, the kind, helping hand, the warm heart, patience, diligence, humility, and friendliness attain to honour; for here these are the most useful qualities, and almost the only means of supporting the burden of existence. Slave-morality is essentially the morality of utility. Here is the seat of the origin of the famous antithesis 'good' and 'evil': power and dangerousness are assumed to reside in the evil, a certain dreadfulness, subtlety, and strength, which do not admit of being despised. According to slave-morality, therefore, the 'evil' man arouses fear; according to master-morality, it is precisely the 'good' man who arouses fear and seeks to arouse it, while the bad man is regarded as the despicable being. The contrast attains its maximum when, in accordance with the logical consequences of slave-morality, a shade of depreciation – it may be slight and well-intentioned – at last attaches itself to the 'good' man of this morality; because, according to the servile mode of thought, the good man must in any case be the *safe* man: he is good-natured, easily deceived, perhaps a little stupid, *un bonhomme*. Everywhere that slave-morality gains the ascendancy, language shows a tendency to approximate the significations of the words 'good' and 'stupid'. A last fundamental difference: the desire for *freedom*, the instinct for happiness and the refinements of the feeling of liberty belong as necessarily to slave-morals and morality, as artifice and enthusiasm in reverence and devotion are the regular symptoms of an aristocratic mode of thinking and estimating. Hence we can understand without further detail why love *as a passion* – it is our European specialty – must absolutely be of noble origin; as is well known, its invention is due to the Provencal poet-cavaliers, those brilliant, ingenious men of the '*gai saber*',[3] to whom Europe owes so much, and almost owes itself.

261. Vanity is one of the things which are perhaps most difficult for a noble man to understand: he will be tempted to deny it, where another kind of man thinks he sees it self-evidently. The problem for him is to represent to his mind beings who seek to arouse a good opinion of themselves which they themselves do not possess – and consequently also do not 'deserve' – and who yet *believe* in this good opinion

3. Old Provençal: 'gay knowledge' or 'gay science', the art of composing love poetry; especially the art of the Provençal troubadours.

afterwards. This seems to him on the one hand such bad taste and so self-disrespectful, and on the other hand so grotesquely unreasonable, that he would like to consider vanity an exception, and is doubtful about it in most cases when it is spoken of. He will say, for instance: 'I may be mistaken about my value, and on the other hand may nevertheless demand that my value should be acknowledged by others precisely as I rate it – that, however, is not vanity (but self-conceit, or, in most cases, that which is called 'humility', and also 'modesty').' Or he will even say: 'For many reasons I can delight in the good opinion of others, perhaps because I love and honour them, and rejoice in all their joys, perhaps also because their good opinion endorses and strengthens my belief in my own good opinion, perhaps because the good opinion of others, even in cases where I do not share it, is useful to me, or gives promise of usefulness – all this, however, is not vanity.' The man of noble character must first bring it home forcibly to his mind, especially with the aid of history, that, from time immemorial, in all social strata in any way dependent, the ordinary man *was* only that which he *passed for* – not being at all accustomed to fix values, he did not assign even to himself any other value than that which his master assigned to him (it is the peculiar *right of masters* to create values). It may be looked upon as the result of an extraordinary atavism, that the ordinary man, even at present, is still always *waiting* for an opinion about himself, and then instinctively submitting himself to it; yet by no means only to a 'good' opinion, but also to a bad and unjust one (think, for instance, of the greater part of the self-appreciations and self-depreciations which believing women learn from their confessors, and which in general the believing Christian learns from his Church). In fact, conformably to the slow rise of the democratic social order (and its cause, the blending of the blood of masters and slaves), the originally noble and rare impulse of the masters to assign a value to themselves, and to 'think well' of themselves, will now be more and more encouraged and extended; but it has at all times an older, ampler, and more radically ingrained propensity opposed to it – and in the phenomenon of 'vanity' this older propensity overmasters the younger. The vain person rejoices over *every* good opinion which he hears about himself (quite apart from the point of view of its usefulness, and equally regardless of its truth or falsehood), just as he suffers from every bad opinion: for he subjects himself to both, he feels himself subjected to both, by that oldest instinct of subjection which breaks forth in him. It is 'the slave' in the vain man's blood, the remains of the slave's craftiness – and how much of the 'slave' is still left in woman, for instance! – which seeks to *seduce* to good opinions of itself; it is the slave, too, who immediately afterwards falls prostrate himself before these opinions, as though he had not called them forth. And to repeat it again: vanity is an atavism.

262. A *species* originates, and a type becomes established and strong in the long struggle with essentially constant *unfavourable* conditions. On the other hand, it is known by the experience of breeders that species which receive super-abundant nourishment, and in general a surplus of protection and care, immediately tend in the most marked way to develop variations, and are fertile in prodigies and monstrosities (also in monstrous vices). Now look at an aristocratic commonwealth, say an ancient Greek polis, or Venice, as a voluntary or involuntary contrivance for the purpose of *rearing* human beings; there are there men beside one another, thrown upon their own resources, who want to make their species prevail, chiefly because they *must* prevail, or else run the terrible danger of being exterminated. The favour, the super-abundance, the protection are there lacking under which variations are fostered; the species needs itself as species, as something which, precisely by virtue of its hardness, its uniformity, and simplicity of structure, can in general prevail and make itself permanent in constant struggle with its neighbours, or with rebellious or rebellion-threatening vassals. The most varied experience teaches it what are the qualities to which it principally owes the fact that it still exists, in spite of all Gods and men, and has hitherto been victorious: these qualities it calls virtues, and these virtues alone it develops to maturity. It does so with severity, indeed it desires severity; every aristocratic morality is intolerant in the

education of youth, in the control of women, in the marriage customs, in the relations of old and young, in the penal laws (which have an eye only for the degenerating): it counts intolerance itself among the virtues, under the name of 'justice'. A type with few, but very marked features, a species of severe, warlike, wisely silent, reserved, and reticent men (and as such, with the most delicate sensibility for the charm and nuances of society) is thus established, unaffected by the vicissitudes of generations; the constant struggle with uniform *unfavourable* conditions is, as already remarked, the cause of a type becoming stable and hard. Finally, however, a happy state of things results, the enormous tension is relaxed; there are perhaps no more enemies among the neighbouring peoples, and the means of life, even of the enjoyment of life, are present in superabundance. With one stroke the bond and constraint of the old discipline severs: it is no longer regarded as necessary, as a condition of existence – if it would continue, it can only do so as a form of *luxury*, as an archaizing *taste*. Variations, whether they be deviations (into the higher, finer, and rarer), or deteriorations and monstrosities, appear suddenly on the scene in the greatest exuberance and splendour; the individual dares to be individual and detach himself. At this turning-point of history there manifest themselves, side by side, and often mixed and entangled together, a magnificent, manifold, virgin-forest-like up-growth and up-striving, a kind of *tropical tempo* in the rivalry of growth, and an extraordinary decay and self-destruction, owing to the savagely opposing and seemingly exploding egoisms, which strive with one another 'for sun and light', and can no longer assign any limit, restraint, or forbearance for themselves by means of the hitherto existing morality. It was this morality itself which piled up the strength so enormously, which bent the bow in so threatening a manner – it is now 'out of date', it is getting 'out of date'. The dangerous and disquieting point has been reached when the greater, more manifold, more comprehensive life *is lived beyond* the old morality; the 'individual' stands out, and is obliged to have recourse to his own law-giving, his own arts and artifices for self-preservation, self-elevation, and self-deliverance. Nothing but new 'Whys', nothing but new 'Hows', no common formulas any longer, misunderstanding and disregard in league with each other, decay, deterioration, and the loftiest desires frightfully entangled, the genius of the race overflowing from all the cornucopias of good and bad, a portentous simultaneousness of Spring and Autumn, full of new charms and mysteries peculiar to the fresh, still inexhausted, still unwearied corruption. Danger is again present, the mother of morality, great danger; this time shifted into the individual, into the neighbour and friend, into the street, into their own child, into their own heart, into all the most personal and secret recesses of their desires and volitions. What will the moral philosophers who appear at this time have to preach?

They discover, these sharp onlookers and loafers, that the end is quickly approaching, that everything around them decays and produces decay, that nothing will endure until the day after tomorrow, except one species of man, the incurably *mediocre*. The mediocre alone have a prospect of continuing and propagating themselves – they will be the men of the future, the sole survivors; 'be like them! become mediocre!' is now the only morality which has still a significance, which still obtains a hearing. But it is difficult to preach this morality of mediocrity! it can never avow what it is and what it desires! it has to talk of moderation and dignity and duty and brotherly love—it will have difficulty *in concealing its irony*!

263. There is an *instinct for rank*, which more than anything else is already the sign of a *high* rank; there is a *delight* in the *nuances* of reverence which leads one to infer noble origin and habits. The refinement, goodness, and loftiness of a soul are put to a perilous test when something passes by that is of the highest rank, but is not yet protected by the awe of authority from obtrusive touches and incivilities: something that goes its way like a living touchstone, undistinguished, undiscovered, and tentative, perhaps voluntarily veiled and disguised. He whose task and practice it is to investigate souls will avail himself of many varieties of this very art to determine the ultimate value of a soul, the unalterable, innate order of rank to which it belongs: he will test it by its *instinct for reverence*. *Difference engendre haine*:[4] the

vulgarity of many a nature spurts up suddenly like dirty water, when any holy vessel, any jewel from closed shrines, any book bearing the marks of great destiny, is brought before it; while on the other hand, there is an involuntary silence, a hesitation of the eye, a cessation of all gestures, by which it is indicated that a soul *feels* the nearness of what is worthiest of respect. The way in which, on the whole, the reverence for the *Bible* has hitherto been maintained in Europe, is perhaps the best example of discipline and refinement of manners which Europe owes to Christianity: books of such profoundness and supreme significance require for their protection an external tyranny of authority, in order to acquire the *period* of thousands of years which is necessary to exhaust and unriddle them. Much has been achieved when the sentiment has been at last instilled into the masses (the shallow-pates and the boobies of every kind) that they are not allowed to touch everything, that there are holy experiences before which they must take off their shoes and keep away the unclean hand – it is almost their highest advance towards humanity. On the contrary, in the so-called cultured classes, the believers in 'modern ideas', nothing is perhaps so repulsive as their lack of shame, the easy insolence of eye and hand with which they touch, taste, and finger everything; and it is possible that even yet there is more *relative* nobility of taste, and

4. Difference engenders hatred.

more tact for reverence among the people, among the lower classes of the people, especially among peasants, than among the newspaper-reading *demimonde* of intellect, the cultured class.

264. It cannot be effaced from a man's soul what his ancestors have preferably and most constantly done: whether they were perhaps diligent economizers attached to a desk and a cash-box, modest and citizen-like in their desires, modest also in their virtues; or whether they were accustomed to commanding from morning till night, fond of rude pleasures and probably of still ruder duties and responsibilities; or whether, finally, at one time or another, they have sacrificed old privileges of birth and possession, in order to live wholly for their faith – for their 'God' – as men of an inexorable and sensitive conscience, which blushes at every compromise. It is quite impossible for a man *not* to have the qualities and predilections of his parents and ancestors in his constitution, whatever appearances may suggest to the contrary. This is the problem of race. Granted that one knows something of the parents, it is admissible to draw a conclusion about the child: any kind of offensive incontinence, any kind of sordid envy, or of clumsy self-vaunting – the three things which together have constituted the genuine plebeian type in all times – such must pass over to the child, as surely as bad blood; and with the help of the best education and culture one will only succeed in *deceiving* with regard to such heredity. And what else

does education and culture try to do nowadays! In our very democratic, or rather, very plebeian age, 'education' and 'culture' *must* be essentially the art of deceiving – deceiving with regard to origin, with regard to the inherited plebeianism in body and soul. An educator who nowadays preached truthfulness above everything else, and called out constantly to his pupils: 'Be true! Be natural! Show yourselves as you are!' – even such a virtuous and sincere ass would learn in a short time to have recourse to the *furca* of Horace, *naturam expellere*: with what results? 'Plebeianism' *usque recurret.*[5]

265. At the risk of displeasing innocent ears, I submit that egoism belongs to the essence of a noble soul, I mean the unalterable belief that to a being such as 'we' other beings must naturally be in subjection, and have to sacrifice themselves. The noble soul accepts the fact of his egoism without question, and also without consciousness of harshness, constraint, or arbitrariness therein, but rather as something that may have its basis in the primary law of things – if he sought a designation for it he would say: 'It is justice itself'. He acknowledges under certain circumstances, which made him hesitate at first, that there are other equally privileged ones; as soon as he has settled this question of rank, he moves among those equals and equally privileged ones with the same assurance, as

---

5. *Naturam expellas furca, tamen usque recurret*: 'you can drive nature with a pitchfork, but she will keep coming back' - Horace, *Epistles*, I. x. 24.

regards modesty and delicate respect, which he enjoys in intercourse with himself – in accordance with an innate heavenly mechanism which all the stars understand. It is an *additional* instance of his egoism, this artfulness and self-limitation in intercourse with his equals – every star is a similar egoist; he honours *himself* in them, and in the rights which he concedes to them, he has no doubt that the exchange of honours and rights, as the *essence* of all intercourse, belongs also to the natural condition of things. The noble soul gives as he takes, prompted by the passionate and sensitive instinct of requital, which is at the root of his nature. The notion of 'favour' has, *inter pares*,[6] neither significance nor good repute; there may be a sublime way of letting gifts as it were light upon one from above, and of drinking them thirstily like dew-drops; but for those arts and displays the noble soul has no aptitude. His egoism hinders him here: in general, he looks 'aloft' unwillingly – he looks either *forward*, horizontally and deliberately, or downwards – *he knows that he is on a height*.

266. 'One can only truly esteem him who does not *look out for* himself' – Goethe to Rath Schlosser.

267. The Chinese have a proverb which mothers even teach their children: '*Siao-sin*' ('*make thy heart small*'). This is the essentially fundamental tendency in latter-day civilizations. I have no doubt that an

6. Among equals.

ancient Greek, also, would first of all remark the self-dwarfing in us Europeans of today – in this respect alone we should immediately be 'distasteful' to him.

268. What, after all, is ignobleness? Words are vocal symbols for ideas; ideas, however, are more or less definite mental symbols for frequently returning and concurring sensations, for groups of sensations. It is not sufficient to use the same words in order to understand one another: we must also employ the same words for the same kind of internal experiences, we must in the end have experiences *in common*. On this account the people of one nation understand one another better than those belonging to different nations, even when they use the same language; or rather, when people have lived long together under similar conditions (of climate, soil, danger, requirement, toil) there *originates* therefrom an entity that 'understands itself' – namely, a nation. In all souls a like number of frequently recurring experiences have gained the upper hand over those occurring more rarely: about these matters people understand one another rapidly and always more rapidly – the history of language is the history of a process of abbreviation; on the basis of this quick comprehension people always unite closer and closer. The greater the danger, the greater is the need of agreeing quickly and readily about what is necessary; not to misunderstand one another in danger – that is what cannot at all be dispensed with in intercourse. Also in all loves and friendships one has the

experience that nothing of the kind continues when the discovery has been made that in using the same words, one of the two parties has feelings, thoughts, intuitions, wishes, or fears different from those of the other. (The fear of the 'eternal misunderstanding': that is the good genius which so often keeps persons of different sexes from too hasty attachments, to which sense and heart prompt them – and *not* some Schopenhauerian 'genius of the species'!) Whichever groups of sensations within a soul awaken most readily, begin to speak, and give the word of command – these decide as to the general order of rank of its values, and determine ultimately its list of desirable things. A man's estimates of value betray something of the *structure* of his soul, and wherein it sees its conditions of life, its intrinsic needs. Supposing now that necessity has from all time drawn together only such men as could express similar requirements and similar experiences by similar symbols, it results on the whole that the easy *communicability* of need, which implies ultimately the undergoing only of average and *common* experiences, must have been the most potent of all the forces which have hitherto operated upon mankind. The more similar, the more ordinary people, have always had and are still having the advantage; the more select, more refined, more unique, and difficultly comprehensible, are liable to stand alone; they succumb to accidents in their isolation, and seldom propagate themselves. One must appeal to immense opposing forces, in order to thwart this natural, all-too-natural *progressus in simile*,[7] the evolution of man to the similar, the ordinary, the average, the gregarious—to the *ignoble*!

...

269. Alas! what are you, after all, my written and painted thoughts! Not long ago you were so variegated, young and malicious, so full of thorns and secret spices, that you made me sneeze and laugh—and now? You have already doffed your novelty, and some of you, I fear, are ready to become truths, so immortal do they look, so pathetically honest, so tedious! And was it ever otherwise? What then do we write and paint, we mandarins with Chinese brush, we immortalisers of things which *lend* themselves to writing, what are we alone capable of painting? Alas, only that which is just about to fade and begins to lose its odour! Alas, only exhausted and departing storms and belated yellow sentiments! Alas, only birds strayed and fatigued by flight, which now let themselves be captured with the hand – with *our* hand! We immortalize what cannot live and fly much longer, things only which are exhausted and mellow! And it is only for your *afternoon*, you, my written and painted thoughts, for which alone I have colours, many colours, perhaps, many variegated softenings, and fifty yellows and browns and greens and reds; but nobody will divine thereby how ye

7. Progression towards the same.

looked in your morning, you sudden sparks and marvels of my solitude, you, my old, beloved – *evil* thoughts!

10

RALPH WALDO EMERSON, SPIRITUAL LAWS

INTRODUCTION

What if, despite all the cynicism and hypocrisy we see around us, there were still a reason to be confident that we can tap into a source of universal power – simply by living life as one's own man?

The great American transcendentalist philosopher, Ralph Waldo Emerson, thought that there was.

Emerson's beliefs were always considered radical. Strongly influenced by the ancient Indian classics, the *Bhagavad Gita* and the Vedanta, as well as Quakerism and German philosophy, Emerson believed that all things were connected to God and, therefore, all things were divine. Life was usually experienced as a series of incomplete and partial glimpses of reality, he thought, whereas in fact each tangible being is merely one aspect of a resplendent underlying unity. The power of that underlying unity – that 'soul of the whole' as Emerson calls it – is accessible to all of us.

Of course, if there really were some way of accessing the power of the universe, we would naturally want to have some guidance as to how to do that.

Emerson's essay, 'Spiritual Laws', attempts to provide that guidance. He does not himself list the laws to which he refers in the title; he wanted to inspire far more than he wanted to enumerate. That humbler task falls to us. So – what laws can be discerned?

Emerson understands that the universe is experienced differently according to a man's fundamental nature. Our genius or nature determines for us the character of the universe because the universe responds and becomes meaningful in answer to it. We attract experiences that are significant to us in the same way that a magnet attracts iron filings. The right thing for us is that which corresponds to our own inner constitution, rather than that which we choose, since choice is only 'a partial act of hands, eyes, and appetites rather than the whole being'. Our character is constantly making itself known and is impossible to hide: it reveals itself in our smallest acts and dispays itself in our very demeanour.

Emerson also understands that, as one aspect of the infinite responsiveness of the universe, it leaves every man to 'set his own rate' – and unfailingly accepts his own self-assessment. It is for ourselves to attribute our own value to our work and deeds. Work has meaning, and becomes vocation, insofar as it is an outlet for our character and aims. At the same time, extraordinary success comes from the self-negation which allows for creative energy to find its outlet in the world.

Finally, Emerson understands that everything stems from the inner man. It is not in activity or making external changes that we recreate ourselves. The epochs of our lives are determined 'in a silent thought by the wayside as we walk'. We may admire the great institutions of the world but we forget that each of them was initiated, at one point, by a single thought.

Emerson was widely considered to have been the most influential writer of nineteenth-century America. For the modern reader, Emerson's value lies in what he himself identified as the central doctrine of his work – 'the infinitude of the private man'. Mass man, man as an economic unit, man as a 'human resource' – these bugbears of the twentieth and twenty-first centuries would have been anathema to Emerson. Instead, Emerson reminds us of our dignity, our expansiveness, and our power to begin the process of regenerating the universe from within.

SPIRITUAL LAWS

When the act of reflection takes place in the mind, when we look at ourselves in the light of thought, we discover that our life is embosomed in beauty. Behind us, as we go, all things assume pleasing forms, as clouds do far off. Not only things familiar and stale, but even the tragic and terrible are comely as they take their place in the pictures of memory. The river-bank, the weed at the water-side, the old house, the foolish person, however neglected in the passing, have a grace in the past. Even the corpse that has lain in the chambers has added a solemn ornament to the house. The soul will not know either deformity or pain. If in the hours of clear reason we should speak the severest truth, we should say that we had never made a sacrifice. In these hours the mind seems so great that nothing can be taken from us that seems much. All loss, all pain, is particular; the universe remains to the heart unhurt. Neither vexations nor calamities abate our trust. No man ever stated his griefs as lightly as he might. Allow for exaggeration in the most patient and sorely ridden hack that ever was driven. For it is only the finite that has wrought and suffered; the infinite lies stretched in smiling repose.

The intellectual life may be kept clean and healthful if man will live the life of nature and not import into his mind difficulties which are none of his. No man need be perplexed in his speculations. Let him do and say what strictly belongs to him, and though very ignorant of books, his nature shall not yield him any intellectual obstructions and doubts. Our young people are diseased with the theological problems of original sin, origin of evil, predestination and the like. These never presented a practical difficulty to any man, never darkened across any man's road who did not go out of his way to seek them. These are the soul's mumps and measles and whooping-coughs, and those who have not caught them cannot describe their health or prescribe the cure. A simple mind will not know these enemies. It is quite another thing that he should be able to give account of his faith and expound to another the theory of his self-union and freedom. This requires rare gifts. Yet without this self-knowledge there may be a sylvan strength and integrity in that which he is. 'A few strong instincts and a few plain rules' suffice us.

My will never gave the images in my mind the rank they now take. The regular course of studies, the years of academical and professional education have not yielded me better facts than some idle books under the bench at the Latin School. What we do not call education is more precious than that which we call so. We form no guess, at the time of receiving a thought, of its comparative value. And education often wastes its effort in attempts to thwart and balk this natural magnetism, which is sure to select what belongs to it.

In like manner our moral nature is vitiated by any interference of our will. People represent virtue as a struggle, and take to themselves great airs upon their attainments, and the question is everywhere vexed, when a noble nature is commended, whether the man is not better who strives with temptation. But there is no merit in the matter. Either God is there or he is not there. We love characters in proportion as they are impulsive and spontaneous. The less a man thinks or knows about his virtues the better we like him. Timoleon's victories are the best victories, which ran and flowed like Homer's verses, Plutarch said. When we see a soul whose acts are all regal, graceful, and pleasant as roses, we must thank God that such things can be and are, and not turn sourly on the angel and say 'Crump is a better man with his grunting resistance to all his native devils.'

Not less conspicuous is the preponderance of nature over will in all practical life. There is less intention in history than we ascribe to it. We impute deep-laid far-sighted plans to Caesar and Napoleon; but the best of their power was in nature, not in them. Men of an extraordinary success, in their honest moments, have always sung, 'Not unto us, not unto us.' According to the faith of their times they have built altars to Fortune, or to Destiny, or to St. Julian. Their success lay in their parallelism to the course of thought, which found in them an unobstructed channel; and the wonders of which they were the visible conductors seemed to the eye their deed. Did the wires generate the galvanism? It is even true that there was less in them on which they could reflect than in another, as the virtue of a pipe is to be smooth and hollow. That which externally seemed will and immovableness was willingness and self-annihilation. Could Shakespeare give a theory of Shakespeare? Could ever a man of prodigious mathematical genius convey to others any insight into his methods? If he could communicate that secret it would instantly lose its exaggerated value, blending with the daylight and the vital energy the power to stand and to go.

The lesson is forcibly taught by these observations that our life might be much easier and simpler than we make it; that the world might be a happier place than it is; that there is no need of struggles, convulsions, and despairs, of the wringing of the hands and the gnashing of the teeth; that we miscreate our own evils. We interfere with the optimism of nature; for whenever we get this vantage-ground of the past, or of a wiser mind in the present, we are able to discern that we are begirt with laws which execute themselves.

The face of external nature teaches the same lesson. Nature will not have us fret and fume. She does not like our benevolence or our learning much better than she likes our frauds and wars. When we come out of the caucus, or the bank, or the Abolition-convention, or the Temperance-meeting, or the Transcendental club into the fields and woods, she says to us, 'So hot? my little Sir.'

We are full of mechanical actions. We must needs intermeddle and have things in our own way, until the sacrifices and virtues of society are odious. Love should make joy; but our benevolence is unhappy. Our Sunday-schools and churches and pauper-societies are yokes to the neck. We pain ourselves to please nobody. There are natural ways of arriving at the same ends at which these aim, but do not arrive. Why should all virtue work in one and the same way? Why should all give dollars? It is very inconvenient to us country folk, and we do not think any good will come of it. We have not dollars; merchants have; let them give them. Farmers will give corn; poets will sing; women will sew; laborers will lend a hand; the children will bring flowers. And why drag this dead weight of a Sunday-school over the whole Christendom? It is natural and beautiful that childhood should inquire and maturity should teach; but it is time enough to answer questions when they are asked. Do not shut up the young people against their will in a pew and force the children to ask them questions for an hour against their will.

...

I say, do not choose; but that is a figure of speech by which I would distinguish what is commonly called choice among men, and which is a partial act, the choice of the hands, of the eyes, of the appetites, and not a whole act of the man. But that which I call right or goodness, is the choice of my constitution; and that which I call heaven, and inwardly aspire after, is the state or circumstance desirable to my constitution; and the action which I in all my years tend to do, is the work for my faculties. We must hold a man amenable to reason for the choice of his daily craft or profession. It is not an excuse any longer for his deeds that they are the custom of his trade. What business has he with an evil trade? Has he not a calling in his character?

Each man has his own vocation. The talent is the call. There is one direction in which all space is open to him. He has faculties silently inviting him thither to endless exertion. He is like a ship in a river; he runs against obstructions on every side but one, on that side all obstruction is taken away and he sweeps serenely over a deepening channel into an infinite sea. This talent and this call depend on his organization, or the mode in which the general soul incarnates itself in him. He inclines to do something which is easy to him and good when it is done, but which no other man can do. He has no rival. For the more truly he consults his own powers, the more difference will his work exhibit from the work of any other. His ambition is exactly proportioned to his powers. The height of the pinnacle is determined by the breadth of the base. Every man has this call of the power to do somewhat unique, and no man has any other call. The pretence that he has another call, a summons by name and personal election and outward 'signs that mark him extraordinary, and not in the roll of common men,' is fanaticism, and betrays obtuseness to perceive that there is one mind in all the individuals, and no respect of persons therein.

By doing his work he makes the need felt which he can supply, and creates the taste by which he is enjoyed. By doing his own work he unfolds himself. It is the vice of our public speaking that it has not abandonment. Somewhere, not only every orator but every man should let out all the length of all the reins; should find or make a frank and hearty expression of what force and meaning is in him. The common experience is that the man fits himself as well as he can to the customary details of that work or trade he falls into, and tends it as a dog turns a spit. Then is he a part of the machine he moves; the man is lost. Until he can manage to communicate himself to others in his full stature and proportion, he does not yet find his vocation. He must find in that an outlet for his character, so that he may justify his work to their eyes. If the labor is mean, let him by his thinking and character make it liberal. Whatever he knows and thinks, whatever in his apprehension is worth doing, that let him communicate, or men will never know and honor him aright. Foolish, whenever you take the meanness and formality of that thing you do, instead of converting it into the obedient spiracle of your character and aims.

We like only such actions as have already long had the praise of men, and do not perceive that any thing man can do may be divinely done. We think greatness entailed or organized in some places or duties, in certain offices or occasions, and do not see that Paganini can extract rapture from a catgut, and Eulenstein from a jews-harp, and a nimble-fingered lad out of shreds of paper with his scissors, and Landseer out of swine, and the hero out of the pitiful habitation and company in which he was hidden. What we call obscure condition or vulgar society is that condition and society whose poetry is not yet written, but which you shall presently make as enviable and renowned as any. In our estimates let us take a lesson from kings. The parts of hospitality, the connection of families, the impressiveness of death, and a thousand other things, royalty makes its own estimate of, and a royal mind will. To make habitually a new estimate—that is elevation.

What a man does, that he has. What has he to do with hope or fear? In himself is his might. Let him regard no good as solid but that which is in his nature and which must grow out of him as long as he exists. The goods of fortune may come and go like summer leaves; let him scatter them on every wind as the momentary signs of his infinite productiveness.

He may have his own. A man's genius, the quality that differences him from every other, the susceptibility to one class of influences, the selection of what is fit for him, the rejection of what is unfit, determines for him the character of the universe. A man is a method, a progressive arrangement; a selecting principle, gathering his like to him wherever he goes. He takes only his own out of the multiplicity that sweeps and circles round him. He is like one of those booms which are set out from the shore on rivers to catch drift-wood, or like the loadstone amongst splinters of steel. Those facts, words, persons, which dwell in his memory without his being able to say why, remain because they have a relation to him not less real for being as yet unapprehended. They are symbols of value to him as they can interpret parts of his consciousness which he would vainly seek words for in the conventional images of books and other minds. What attracts my attention shall have it, as I will go to the man who knocks at my door, whilst a thousand persons as worthy go by it, to whom I give no regard. It is enough that these particulars speak to me. A few anecdotes, a few traits of character, manners, face, a few incidents, have an emphasis in your memory out of all proportion to their apparent significance if you measure them by the ordinary standards. They relate to your gift. Let them have their weight, and do not reject them and cast about for illustration and facts more usual in literature. What your heart thinks great is great. The soul's emphasis is always right.

Over all things that are agreeable to his nature and genius the man has the highest right. Everywhere he may take what belongs to his spiritual estate, nor can he take anything else though all doors were open, nor can all the force of men hinder him from taking so much. It is vain to attempt to keep a secret from one who has a right to know it. It will tell itself. That mood into which a friend can bring us is his dominion over us. To the thoughts of that state of mind he has a right. All the secrets of that state of mind he can compel. This is a law which statesmen use in practice. All the terrors of the French Republic, which held Austria in awe, were unable to command her diplomacy. But Napoleon sent to Vienna Monsieur de Narbonne, one of the old noblesse, with the morals, manners, and name of that interest, saying that it was indispensable to send to the old aristocracy of Europe men of the same connection, which, in fact, constitutes a sort of free-masonry. Monsieur de Narbonne in less than a fortnight penetrated all the secrets of the imperial cabinet.

Nothing seems so easy as to speak and to be understood. Yet a man may come to find that the strongest of defences and of ties—that he has been understood; and he who has received an opinion may come to find it the most inconvenient of bonds.

If a teacher have any opinion which he wishes to conceal, his pupils will become as fully indoctrinated into that as into any which he publishes. If you pour water into a vessel twisted into coils and angles, it is vain to say, I will pour it only into this or that—it will find its level in all. Men feel and act the consequences of your doctrine without being able to show how they follow. Show us an arc of the curve, and a good mathematician will find out the whole figure. We are always reasoning from the seen to the unseen. Hence the perfect intelligence that subsists between wise men of remote ages. A man cannot bury his meanings so deep in his book but time and like-minded men will find them. Plato had a secret doctrine, had he? What secret can he conceal from the eyes of Bacon? of Montaigne? of Kant? Therefore, Aristotle said of his works, 'They are published and not published.'

No man can learn what he has not preparation for learning, however near to his eyes is the object. A chemist may tell his most precious secrets to a carpenter, and he shall be never the wiser—the secrets he would not utter to a chemist for an estate. God screens us evermore from premature ideas. Our eyes are holden that we cannot see things that stare us in the face, until the hour arrives when the mind is ripened; then we behold them, and the time when we saw them not is like a dream.

Not in nature but in man is all the beauty and worth he sees. The world is very empty, and is indebted to this gilding, exalting soul for all its pride. 'Earth fills her lap with splendors' not her own. The vale of Tempe, Tivoli, and Rome are earth and water, rocks and sky. There are as good earth and water in a thousand places, yet how unaffecting!

...

He may set his own rate. It is a maxim worthy of all acceptation that a man may have that allowance he takes. Take the place and attitude which belong to you, and all men acquiesce. The world must be just. It leaves every man, with profound unconcern, to set his own rate. Hero or driveller, it meddles not in the matter. It will certainly accept your own measure of your doing and being, whether you sneak about and deny your own name, or whether you see your work produced to the concave sphere of the heavens, one with the revolution of the stars.

The same reality pervades all teaching. The man may teach by doing, and not otherwise. If he can communicate himself he can teach, but not by words. He teaches who gives, and he learns who receives. There is no teaching until the pupil is brought into the same state or principle in which you are; a transfusion takes place; he is you and you are he; then is a teaching, and by no unfriendly chance or bad company can he ever quite lose the benefit. But your propositions run out of one ear as they ran in at the other. We see it advertised that Mr. Grand will deliver an oration on the Fourth of July, and Mr. Hand before the Mechanics' Association, and we do not go thither, because we know that these gentlemen will not communicate their own character and experience to the company. If we had reason to expect such a confidence we should go through all inconvenience and opposition. The sick would be carried in litters. But a public oration is an escapade, a non-committal, an apology, a gag, and not a communication, not a speech, not a man.

A like nemesis presides over all intellectual works. We have yet to learn that the thing uttered in words is not therefore affirmed. It must affirm itself, or no forms of logic or of oath can give it evidence. The sentence must also contain its own apology for being spoken.

...

In like manner the effect of every action is measured by the depth of the sentiment from which it proceeds. The great man knew not that he was great. It took a century or two for that fact to appear. What he did, he did because he must; it was the most natural thing in the world, and grew out of the circumstances of the moment. But now, every thing he did, even to the lifting of his finger or the eating of bread, looks large, all-related, and is called an institution.

These are the demonstrations in a few particulars of the genius of nature; they show the direction of the stream. But the stream is blood; every drop is alive. Truth has not single victories; all things are its organs—not only dust and stones, but errors and lies. The laws of disease, physicians say, are as beautiful as the laws of health. Our philosophy is affirmative and readily accepts the testimony of negative facts, as every shadow points to the sun. By a divine necessity every fact in nature is constrained to offer its testimony.

Human character evermore publishes itself. The most fugitive deed and word, the mere air of doing a thing, the intimated purpose, expresses character. If you act you show character; if you sit still, if you sleep, you show it. You think because you have spoken nothing when others spoke, and have given no opinion on the times, on the church, on slavery, on marriage, on socialism, on secret societies, on the college, on parties and persons, that your verdict is still expected with curiosity as a reserved wisdom. Far otherwise; your silence answers very loud. You have no oracle to utter, and your fellow-men have learned that you cannot help them; for oracles speak. Doth not Wisdom cry and Understanding put forth her voice?

Dreadful limits are set in nature to the powers of dissimulation. Truth tyrannizes over the unwilling members of the body. Faces never lie, it is said. No man need be deceived who will study the changes of expression. When a man speaks the truth in the spirit of truth, his eye is as clear as the heavens. When he has base ends and speaks falsely, the eye is muddy and sometimes asquint.

I have heard an experienced counsellor say that he never feared the effect upon a jury of a lawyer who does not believe in his heart that his client ought to have a verdict. If he does not believe it his unbelief will appear to the jury, despite all his protestations, and will become their unbelief. This is that law whereby a work of art, of whatever kind, sets us in the same state of mind wherein the artist was when he made it. That which we do not believe we cannot adequately say, though we may repeat the words never so often. It was this conviction which Swedenborg expressed when he described a group of persons in the spiritual world endeavoring in vain to articulate a proposition which they did not believe; but they could not, though they twisted and folded their lips even to indignation.

A man passes for that he is worth. Very idle is all curiosity concerning other people's estimate of us, and all fear of remaining unknown is not less so. If a man know that he can do anything—that he can do it better than any one else—he has a pledge of the acknowledgment of that fact by all persons. The world is full of judgment days, and into every assembly that a man enters, in every action he attempts, he is gauged and stamped. In every troop of boys that whoop and run in each yard and square, a newcomer is as well and accurately weighed in the course of a few days and stamped with his right number, as if he had undergone a formal trial of his strength, speed, and temper. A stranger comes from a distant school, with better dress, with trinkets in his pockets, with airs and pretensions; an older boy says to himself, 'It's of no use; we shall find him out to-morrow.' 'What has he done?' is the divine question which searches men and transpierces every false reputation. A fop may sit in any chair of the world nor be distinguished for his hour from Homer and Washington; but there need never be any doubt concerning the respective ability of human beings. Pretension may sit still, but cannot act. Pretension never feigned an act of real greatness. Pretension never wrote an Iliad, nor drove back Xerxes, nor christianized the world, nor abolished slavery.

As much virtue as there is, so much appears; as much goodness as there is, so much reverence it commands. All the devils respect virtue. The high, the generous, the self-devoted sect will always instruct and command mankind. Never was a sincere word utterly lost. Never a magnanimity fell to the ground, but there is some heart to greet and accept it unexpectedly. A man passes for that he is worth. What he is engraves itself on his face, on his form, on his fortunes, in letters of light. Concealment avails him nothing, boasting nothing. There is confession in the glances of our eyes, in our smiles, in salutations, and the grasp of hands. His sin bedaubs him, mars all his good impression. Men know not why they do not trust him, but they do not trust him. His vice glasses his eye, cuts lines of mean expression in his cheek, pinches the nose, sets the mark of the beast on the back of the head, and writes O fool! fool! on the forehead of a king.

If you would not be known to do anything, never do it. A man may play the fool in the drifts of a desert, but every grain of sand shall seem to see. He may be a solitary eater, but he cannot keep his foolish counsel. A broken complexion, a swinish look, ungenerous acts and the want of due knowledge—all blab. Can a cook, a Chiffinch, an Iachimo be mistaken for Zeno or Paul? Confucius exclaimed, 'How can a man be concealed? How can a man be concealed?'

On the other hand, the hero fears not that if he withhold the avowal of a just and brave act it will go unwitnessed and unloved. One knows it—himself—and is pledged by it to sweetness of peace and to nobleness of aim which will prove in the end a better proclamation of it than the relating of the incident. Virtue is the adherence in action to the nature of things, and the nature of things makes it prevalent. It consists in a perpetual substitution of being for seeming, and with sublime propriety God is described as saying, I AM.

The lesson which these observations convey is, Be, and not seem. Let us acquiesce. Let us take our bloated nothingness out of the path of the divine circuits. Let us unlearn our wisdom of the world. Let us lie low in the Lord's power and learn that truth alone makes rich and great.

If you visit your friend, why need you apologize for not having visited him, and waste his time and deface your own act? Visit him now. Let him feel that the highest love has come to see him, in thee its lowest organ. Or why need you torment yourself and friend by secret self-reproaches that you have not assisted him or complimented him with gifts and salutations heretofore? Be a gift and a benediction. Shine with real light and not with the borrowed reflection of gifts. Common men are apologies for men; they bow the head, excuse themselves with prolix reasons, and accumulate appearances because the substance is not.

We are full of these superstitions of sense, the worship of magnitude. We call the poet inactive, because he is not a president, a merchant, or a porter.

We adore an institution, and do not see that it is founded on a thought which we have. But real action is in silent moments. The epochs of our life are not in the visible facts of our choice of a calling, our marriage, our acquisition of an office, and the like, but in a silent thought by the wayside as we walk; in a thought which revises our entire manner of life and says, 'Thus hast thou done, but it were better thus.' And all our after years, like menials, serve and wait on this, and according to their ability execute its will. ...

Conclusion

'May you live in interesting times' is said to be the English translation of a Chinese curse. While its provenance is in doubt – no Chinese source has been found, and the saying may, in fact, have emanated from the correspondence of British statesman Sir Austen Chamberlain – the meaning is clear. It's better to live in uneventful and uninteresting times than in interesting times – because interesting times are also dangerous times.

Interesting times these are. What we are experiencing in the Western world is the collapse of the post-World War II consensus. For around 70 years, and especially since the fall of the Soviet Union in 1991, the victors of that conflict have had almost complete free rein to remold the world in their own image. The result has been a world that those who fought and died could never have expected and would probably have found alien and unattractive. It has been a world increasingly dominated by a narrow technocratic elite, totalized media, intrusive global surveillance, active censorship, and criminalization of thought and speech. It has been a world that appears to be marching progressively onwards towards the future predicted in Orwell's 1984. That this is not acknowledged by the primary beneficiaries of the current arrangements is neither here nor there.

From where we stand now, it is not difficult to see that the primary engine of change has been the openness of communication made possible by the Internet. For the first time in human history, ordinary people have been able to find out for themselves the truth or falsity of virtually any alleged fact, whether contemporary or historical. This has been a bracing experience for the guardians and gatekeepers of the old regime: governments and international organizations, the professions, mainstream media, and the universities are no longer treated with the deference they once enjoyed. There have been, and will continue to be, attempts to turn back the clock. But the cat is out of the bag.

We now have a choice.

The first option is to double down. We can attempt to entrench the worldview that we have inherited. This would mean the comfort of knowing that our hitherto shared assumptions about society, politics, and history will be defended. It would also mean increased controls: more regulation, more surveillance, and more restrictions on freedom of thought and speech. The establishment's voice would become that much more shrill and its fist would become that much heavier.

The second option is to accept the inevitability of change. It is to undergo a degree of disruption as certain of our beliefs and values are recognized to be no longer convincing or sustainable. But it is also to take part in the process of building a new and hopefully better world.

Classic works such as those found in this book will serve as an anchor during these times of change. They provide thoughtful reflection as a corrective and counterbalance to the more extreme belief systems that surround us. They are also a source of inspiration for renewal. As the ideologies of the twentieth century fail and pass, there will come a time to create new ways of thinking. We cannot as yet know what these new ways of thinking will be. What we can say is that they will be built in some way on the materials passed down to us from our forebears.

George Orwell once said that he who controls the past controls the future.

It is now time to take control of that past and make it our own again.

BIBLIOGRAPHY

Aristotle. *The Nicomachean Ethics of Aristotle.* Translated by
F.H. Peters. 5th ed. London: Kegan Paul, Trench,
Trübner & Co, 1909.

Aurelius, Marcus. *The Meditations of the Emperor Marcus
Aurelius Antoninus.* Translated by George Long. London
and New York: The Chesterfield Society, 1890.

Castiglione, Baldassare. *The Book of the Courtier.* Translated
by Leonard Eckstein Opdyke. New York: Charles
Scribner's Sons, 1903.

Chuang-tzu. *Chuang Tzu: Mystic, Moralist, and Social
Reformer.* Translated by Herbert Giles. London: Bernard
Quaritch, 1889.

Emerson, Ralph Waldo. *Essays: First Series.* Cambridge, MA:
The Riverside Press, 1893.

Gracián, Baltasar. *The Art of Worldly Wisdom.* Translated
by Joseph Jacobs. London and New York: Macmillan &
Co, 1892.

Hazlitt, William. *The Plain Speaker: Opinions on Books, Men,
and Things.* London: Bell & Daldy, 1870.

Machiavelli, Niccolò. *Machiavelli's Prince.* Translated by

W.K. Marriott. London and Toronto: J.M. Dent & Sons and E.P.Dutton & Co, 1908.

Nietzsche, Friedrich. *The Complete Works of Friedrich Nietzsche Volume Twelve: Beyond Good and Evil.* Translated by Helen Zimmern. Edinburgh: The Edinburgh Press, 1909.

Plato. *The Republic of Plato.* Translated by Benjamin Jowett. 3rd ed. London: Oxford University Press, 1888.

ALSO AVAILABLE

CLASSIC POLITICAL PHILOSOPHY FOR THE MODERN MAN

ANDREW LYNN

Classic Political Philosophy for the Modern Man serves three purposes: it provides an introduction to the greatest political philosophers of the Western tradition; it allows these profound thinkers to speak to the assumptions and prejudices of our own era on topics ranging from democracy and human rights to equalism and speech laws; and it brings the most enduringly relevant of their works alive again for the modern reader. There is no better starting point for those who seek a genuinely fresh and insightful view on the major questions of our political existence.

221

CLASSIC SPIRITUALITY FOR THE MODERN MAN

ANDREW LYNN

'The basic premise of this book is that strength and weakness have a spiritual dimension.'

Classic Spirituality for the Modern Man brings the spiritual classics alive so that they can once again serve their original and true purpose: to guide and inspire us as we make our way through life. These works speak to us of the fundamental principles of spiritual wisdom, the mysterious primordial force of the 'Tao', the Buddhist art of maintaining mental and emotional equilibrium, and the essential features of Hindu and Sufi self-cultivation, as well as modern approaches to self-realization. There is no better primer in the art of awakened living.

SHAKESPEARE TALES

ANDREW LYNN

Shakespeare is widely considered to be the greatest playwright the world has known. But it has always been difficult and time-consuming to understand his works.

This series gives you classic prose retellings of the complete works, preserving as far as possible for the modern reader Shakespeare's original language and mood. In this totally new edition, the tales are collected by genre and arranged chronologically. Each genre and each tale is provided with a fresh and insightful introduction. The tales are presented in five volumes: Comedies; Tragedies; Tragicomedies; Roman Tales; and English Histories. They are sumptuously illustrated by Sir John Gilbert.

Perfect for the Shakespeare aficionado, the student, and the general reader. There is no better way to understand the Bard.

CPSIA information can be obtained
at www.ICGtesting.com
Printed in the USA
FSHW022117310820
73463FS